Merry
~ Lauren ~

Love,
Mom

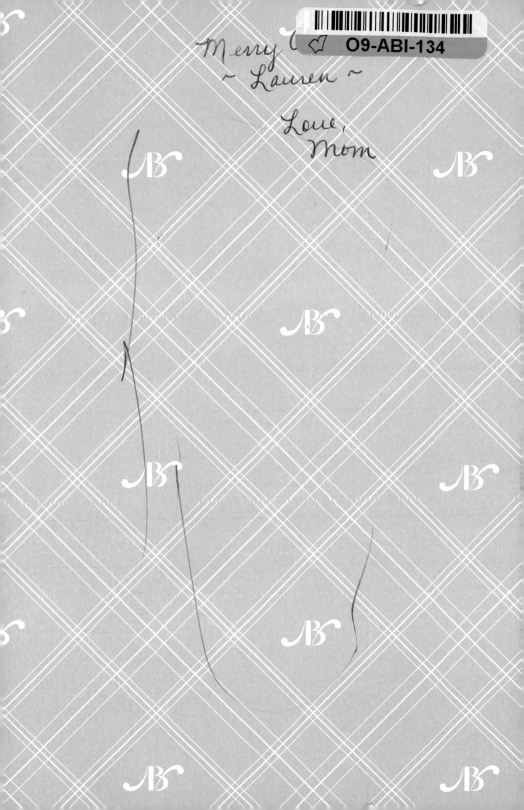

FROM THE PAGES OF

THE COLLECTED POEMS

OF EMILY DICKINSON

If I can stop one heart from breaking,
I shall not live in vain.   (page 8)

Pain has an element of blank;
It cannot recollect
When it began, or if there were
A day when it was not.   (page 16)

Hope is the thing with feathers
That perches in the soul,
And sings the tune without the words,
And never stops at all.   (page 22)

For each ecstatic instant
We must an anguish pay
In keen and quivering ratio
To the ecstasy.   (page 25)

Surgeons must be very careful
When they take the knife!
Underneath their fine incisions
Stirs the culprit,—Life!   (page 28)

Parting is all we know of heaven,
    And all we need of hell.   (page 56)

We never know how high we are
    Till we are called to rise;
And then, if we are true to plan,
    Our statures touch the skies.   (page 56)

It sounded as if the streets were running,
And then the streets stood still.
Eclipse was all we could see at the window,
And awe was all we could feel.   (pages 102–103)

I'll tell you how the sun rose, —
A ribbon at a time.   (page 127)

If certain, when this life was out,
That yours and mine should be,
I'd toss it yonder like a rind,
And taste eternity.   (pages 154–155)

Because I could not stop for Death,
He kindly stopped for me;
The carriage held but just ourselves
And Immortality.   (page 200)

They say that "time assuages", —
    Time never did assuage;
An actual suffering strengthens,
    As sinews do, with age.   (page 233)

Death is the common right
    Of toads and men.   (pages 257–258)

To be alive is power,
Existence in itself.   (page 266)

That Love is all there is,
Is all we know of Love.   (page 312)

THE COLLECTED POEMS OF EMILY DICKINSON

With an Introduction and Notes
By Rachel Wetzsteon

Consulting Editorial Director

George Stade

BARNES & NOBLE CLASSICS
NEW YORK

$\mathcal{B}$

BARNES & NOBLE CLASSICS

NEW YORK

Published by Barnes & Noble Books
122 Fifth Avenue
New York, NY 10011

www.barnesandnoble.com/classics

Emily Dickinson's poems were first published between 1890 and 1891 in three volumes, edited by Thomas Wentworth Higginson and Mabel L. Todd. *The Single Hound* was edited by Dickinson's niece Martha Dickinson Bianchi, and published in 1914.

Published in 2003 by Barnes & Noble Classics with new Introduction, Notes, Biography, Chronology, Inspired By, Comments & Questions, and For Further Reading. Hardcover edition published in 2004.

Introduction, Notes, and For Further Reading
Copyright © 2003 by Rachel Wetzsteon.

Note on Emily Dickinson, The World of Emily Dickinson and Her Poetry, Inspired by Emily Dickinson's Poetry, and Comments & Questions
Copyright © 2003 by Barnes & Noble, Inc.

The Collected Poems of Emily Dickinson
ISBN 1-59308-327-0
LC Control Number 2004108069

Produced and published in conjunction with:
Fine Creative Media, Inc.
322 Eighth Avenue
New York, NY 10001
Michael J. Fine, President and Publisher

Printed in the United States of America
QM
1 3 5 7 9 10 8 6 4 2
FIRST EDITION

EMILY DICKINSON

Emily Dickinson was born on December 10, 1830, in Amherst, Massachusetts, the second child of Emily Norcross and Edward Dickinson. Emily's family was prosperous and well established in Amherst society: Her grandfather, Samuel Fowler Dickinson, was the founder of the prestigious Amherst Academy and a cofounder of Amherst College; her father, Edward, a lawyer and politician, was treasurer of Amherst College. The family lived in Amherst's first brick building, the Homestead, built by Emily's grandfather in 1813. Dickinson grew up in a strict religious household governed mainly by her father, who often censored her reading choices.

She attended Amherst Academy until she was seventeen, and then spent a year at the Mount Holyoke Female Seminary (now Mount Holyoke College). She studied a diversity of subjects, including botany and horticulture, which would become lifelong interests. Among writers she studied, she was particularly inspired by the poet Elizabeth Barrett Browning and the novelist George Eliot. It was during her year at Mount Holyoke that she began to question, and even to voice dissension from, her father's strict religious views.

In 1848, when she was eighteen years old, Dickinson left college and returned to the Homestead, where she lived for the rest of her life. She left home for only a few brief trips to Philadelphia, Washington, D.C., and Boston. It was during a trip to Philadelphia that she met her lifelong friend the Reverend Charles Wadsworth. In 1856 her brother, Austin, married Susan Huntington Gilbert, who would become one of Dickinson's closest friends. The couple moved next door to the Homestead into a house built by Dickinson's father, the Evergreens. At the Evergreens, Dickinson met and began a correspondence with Samuel Bowles, editor of the Springfield *Republican*.

Dickinson wrote the bulk of her nearly 1,800 poems during her years at the Homestead. Five of her poems were printed in the Springfield *Republican*, but Dickinson herself made only one serious attempt at further publication, sending four poems in 1862 to Thomas Wentworth Higginson, poetry editor of the *Atlantic Monthly*. Higginson advised her against publication, saying that the style of her poetry—its unusual rhythm and rhyming—was not commercial. The two continued to correspond, however, and became close friends.

Following the death of her father in 1874, Dickinson became increasingly reclusive, corresponding with friends mainly through letters. She continued writing poetry, and she and her sister, Lavinia, nursed their bedridden mother. Over the next ten years, many of her close friends and family died, including Samuel Bowles, Charles Wadsworth, her mother, and her nephew. In 1884 Dickinson was diagnosed with Bright's disease, a serious kidney disorder. She died from complications of the disease on May 15, 1886.

After Dickinson's death, Lavinia discovered her sister's poems, arranged into little packets bundled with string. She gave them to Higginson and her friend Mabel Loomis Todd for editing. The first of three volumes, titled *Poems*, came out in 1890. A revival of interest in Dickinson's life and poetry occurred in the late 1950s, when Thomas H. Johnson published the first complete edition of Dickinson's poems that was faithful in wording and punctuation to her original manuscripts.

TABLE OF CONTENTS

THE WORLD OF EMILY DICKINSON

AND HER POETRY

1630   Nathaniel Dickinson, the first of Emily Dickinson's family to arrive in America, settles in New England.

1813   Dickinson's grandfather, Samuel Fowler Dickinson, builds the Homestead in Amherst, Massachusetts; the town's first brick house, it will be Dickinson's home for most of her life.

1814   Samuel Fowler Dickinson founds Amherst Academy, which quickly becomes a leading preparatory school in western Massachusetts.

1821   He cofounds the Amherst Collegiate Institution, renamed Amherst College in 1825.

1830   Emily Elizabeth Dickinson is born on December 10, the second child of Edward Dickinson, a prominent lawyer, and Emily Norcross Dickinson.

1835   Edward Dickinson is appointed treasurer of Amherst College.

1840   The Dickinsons move from the Homestead to North Pleasant Street. In the fall Emily and her sister, Lavinia, enter Amherst Academy. Emily is particularly influenced by a teacher, Edward Hitchcock, who emphasizes both religion and science in his lectures and writings.

1847   She attends Mount Holyoke Female Seminary (now Mount Holyoke College) in nearby South Hadley, Massachusetts. At Mount Holyoke, she begins to question her father's Puritanical religious convictions.

1848   In the fall Dickinson leaves Mount Holyoke and moves back into her father's home. She becomes friends with Ben Newton, a young lawyer in her father's office.

1850	Her brother, Austin, begins courting Susan Huntington Gilbert, with whom Dickinson develops an intimate correspondence. Ben Newton gives her a copy of Emerson's poems for Christmas.
1853	Ben Newton's death on March 24 has a profound effect on Dickinson.
1855	Dickinson makes a brief trip with her sister and father to Philadelphia; she meets the Reverend Charles Wadsworth, who becomes a close friend and correspondent. Edward Dickinson repurchases the Homestead; he builds an addition to the house, including a conservatory for Emily's exotic plants.
1856	Austin Dickinson and Susan Gilbert marry; they move into the Evergreens, a house adjacent to the Homestead built for them by Edward as a wedding present.
1858	At the Evergreens, Dickinson meets the literary editor and critic Samuel Bowles, editor of the Springfield *Republican*; they begin a correspondence.
1861	The Civil War breaks out.
1862	Dickinson sends four of her poems to Thomas Wentworth Higginson, poetry editor of the *Atlantic Monthly*. He advises her to regularize the "rough rhythms" and "imperfect rhymes" of her poetry, which he thinks damage its commercial potential. She instead chooses not to publish her works. Dickinson and Higginson begin a correspondence that lasts twenty years.
1864	Dickinson makes two trips to Boston over the next two years to visit an eye specialist. These are the last times she leaves Amherst.
1874	Dickinson's father dies in Boston on June 16. With his death, Dickinson becomes more reclusive, keeping contact with friends and family mainly through letters. She and Lavinia maintain the Homestead and nurse their invalid mother.
1878	Samuel Bowles dies on January 16.
1882	Charles Wadsworth dies on April 1; Dickinson's mother also dies this year, on November 14.

1883	Dickinson's nephew Gilbert, the son of Austin and Susan Gilbert, dies.
1884	On June 14 Dickinson suffers her first attack of Bright's disease, a serious kidney disorder.
1886	Dickinson dies on May 15. Among those attending her funeral is her lifelong friend and mentor Thomas Higginson.
1890	Lavinia finds Dickinson's poems, untitled and bundled into fascicles (sewn paper booklets). She gives them to Higginson and Mabel Loomis Todd, another friend of Dickinson's, for editing. The first of three volumes titled *Poems* is published (the other two are published in 1891 and 1896). The manuscripts are then kept in storage for the next sixty years.
1894	*Letters of Emily Dickinson*, edited by Mabel Todd, is published.
1899	Lavinia dies in 1899.
1914	An edition of Dickinson's poetry — *The Single Hound: Poems of a Lifetime* — edited by her niece Martha Dickinson Bianchi is published.
1955	Thomas H. Johnson rediscovers Dickinson's original poems; he publishes *The Poems of Emily Dickinson*, the first complete collection of her poetry that is free from editorial revisions. The book's publication leads to a renewed interest in Dickinson's poetry.
1963	The Homestead is designated a National Historic Landmark.
1965	Amherst College purchases the Homestead and opens the house as the Emily Dickinson Museum.
1977	The State of Massachusetts establishes the Emily Dickinson Historic District, which includes the Homestead, the Evergreens, and surrounding properties.

INTRODUCTION

Emily Dickinson, writing to the editor Thomas Wentworth Higginson in July 1862, reported that she "had no portrait," but offered the following description in place of one: "Small, like the Wren, and my Hair is bold, like the Chestnut Bur—and my eyes, like the Sherry in the Glass, that the Guest leaves—Would this do just as well?" (*Selected Letters*, edited by Thomas H. Johnson, p. 175; see "For Further Reading"). Despite Dickinson's claim, we do possess one photograph of her—a daguerreotype taken in 1847 or 1848, when she was in her late teens. The image certainly confirms her self-portrait: Her frame is tiny; her shiny hair does indeed sit boldly atop her head; and her dark eyes really do glisten like liquor at the bottom of a glass.

The photograph also suggests many of the rich puzzles and paradoxes that have informed our view of Dickinson since the last decade of the nineteenth century, when readers and critics began to read, study, and obsess over her poems. Dickinson's body, with its delicate hands and slender torso, may resemble the fragile form of someone too weak to venture far from home; but her huge moist eyes stare at us with the wisdom, depth, and longing of a woman who has traveled around the world and come back with stories, not all of them fit for mixed company. She demurely clutches a bouquet of flowers, and a book rests primly at her side; but her full, sensuous lips reveal a person whose thoughts may not always tend toward such tidy subjects as flowers and books. We look away from the photograph intrigued and stirred: What's going on in her mind? How could this slight figure be the author of some of the most passionate love poems, the most searing descriptions of loss, the most haunting religious lyrics ever written?

Emily Elizabeth Dickinson was born in Amherst, Massachusetts, on December 10, 1830, the middle child of Edward and Emily Norcross Dickinson; her brother, Austin, was born in 1829 and her sister, Lavinia, in 1833. Her father, a lawyer, served as treasurer of Amherst College (her grandfather was a cofounder of the college), and also occupied important positions on the General Court of Massachusetts, the Massachusetts State Senate, and the United States House of Representatives. "His Heart," Dickinson wrote in a letter, "was pure and terrible and I think no other like it exists" (*Selected Letters*, p. 223). He was strictly religious (something she would later rebel against), leading the family prayers every day and often censoring her reading; but he also ensured that Dickinson grew up in a household surrounded by books and heated intellectual debates. Her mother was a more shadowy presence; Dickinson wrote that she "does not care for thought" (*Selected Letters*, p. 173); more harshly, she claimed, "I never had a mother. I suppose a mother is one to whom you hurry when you are troubled" (*Letters*, vol. 2, p. 475). Even so, the Dickinsons remained an extremely close-knit family; after her brother, Austin, married, he and his wife settled right next door.

Dickinson attended the coeducational Amherst Academy from the ages of ten to seventeen, and then went on to the Mount Holyoke Female Seminary (now Mount Holyoke College) in nearby South Hadley. She blossomed there into a social and spirited young woman. The most significant event of her stay occurred at a fundamentalist Calvinist revival meeting, when she was asked to stand and declare herself a Christian and refused. After one year at Mount Holyoke she returned in 1848 to Amherst, where she remained, apart from brief trips to Boston, Cambridge, Philadelphia, and Washington, D.C., for the rest of her life.

At school and at home, Dickinson received an excellent education. At the Amherst Academy alone she studied the arts, English literature, rhetoric, philosophy, Latin, French, German, history, geography, classics, and the Bible; she also received a firm grounding in the sciences, mathematics, geology, botany, natural history, physiology, and astronomy. At home the Dickinsons' large and varied library included books by Hawthorne, Emerson, Thoreau, Longfellow, Shakespeare, Keats, the Brownings, the Brontës, and George Eliot, along with Noah Webster's *An American Dictionary of the English Language* — which for Dickinson would prove one of the most important books of all—and a healthy dose of newspapers and romance novels.

During her early twenties, Dickinson began to dress in white, to leave her house only on rare occasions, and to restrict the circle of her acquaintances until it numbered just a few people. Often speaking to visitors through a screen or from an adjoining room, she soon developed a reputation as a town eccentric. The young Mabel Loomis Todd, having recently moved to Amherst with her husband, David, remarked in a letter to her parents about a strange resident:

> I must tell you about the *character* of Amherst. It is a lady whom all the people call the *Myth*. She is a sister of Mr. Dickinson, & seems to be the climax of all the family oddity. She has not been outside her house in fifteen years, except once to see a new church, when she crept out at night, & viewed it by moonlight. No one who calls upon her mother & sister ever sees her, but she allows little children once in a great while, & one at a time, to come in, when she gives them cake or candy, or some nicety, for she is very fond of little ones. But more often she lets down the sweetmeat by a string, out of a window, to them. She dresses wholly in white, & her mind is said to be perfectly wonderful. She writes finely, but no one *ever* sees her. Her sister . . . invited me to come & sing to her mother sometime. . . . People tell me the *myth* will hear every note—she will be near, but unseen. . . . Isn't that like a book? So interesting (Farr, *Emily Dickinson: A Collection of Critical Essays*, p. 20).

One can hardly blame Todd for being fascinated by such an unusual "character." But unfortunately, the "myth" she takes such pleasure in describing influenced our later notions of Dickinson much too heavily. Despite her seclusion, a large number of prominent figures came and went through her house. She also developed deep, though largely epistolary, friendships with several people: the clergyman Charles Wadsworth, whom she met in Philadelphia and described as her "dearest earthly friend"; Samuel Bowles, editor of the Springfield *Republican*; and Judge Otis Phillips Lord of Salem, Massachusetts.

During this time Dickinson also began to write poetry. On April 15, 1862, she read in the *Atlantic Monthly* a "Letter to a Young Contributor," by Thomas Wentworth Higginson. In the letter Higginson, a man of letters, active abolitionist, and early supporter of women's rights offered advice to novice writers about finding an audience for their work. Dickinson sent him four poems, along with a letter inquiring "if my Verse is alive?" and telling Higginson, "Should you feel it breathed—and had you leisure to tell me, I should feel quick gratitude—" (*Selected Letters*, p. 171). Although Higginson may have been politically ahead of his time, his literary tastes were not quite as advanced; he suggested that Dickinson revise her unusual punctuation and syntax. Still, their correspondence, which lasted until the last month of her life, seems to have gone a long way toward helping Dickinson feel part of a greater literary community.

Dickinson experienced her most tumultuous decade during the 1860s, when several events took their toll on her: the outbreak of the Civil War, the changed circumstances of several friends (Bowles was sick in Europe, Wadsworth moved to San Francisco, and Higginson served as an officer in the Union Army), and her own severe eye trouble in 1864 and 1865. After the late 1860s she never again left her home. In April 1862 she wrote mysteriously to Higginson, "I had a terror—since September—I could tell to none—and so I sing, as the Boy does by the Burying Ground—because I am afraid—" (*Selected Letters*, p. 172). These lines certainly confirm Dickinson's difficulties during this time, even though no one knows exactly what her "terror" was. This period, however, proved to be the most productive of Dickinson's life; between 1860 and 1865 she wrote an average of three hundred poems each year.

Although Dickinson never married, her passionate poems, as well as a series of letters that have come to be called "The Master Letters," suggest that she may have been deeply in love at least once; it remains in doubt whether the object of her affection was Charles Wadsworth, Otis Lord, her sister-in-law Susan, or indeed any real person.

The last years of Dickinson's life were sad ones, due to the numerous deaths she experienced. Her father died in 1874, Samuel Bowles in 1878, her nephew Gilbert in 1883, and both Charles

Wadsworth and her mother in 1882. In April 1884 Otis Lord died, and Dickinson herself suffered the first attack of an illness that would prove fatal; she died on May 15, 1886.

With a few exceptions, Dickinson's poems are quite short, and they consist of stanzas written in what is known as common measure, also called common meter: four iambic lines that alternate between four and three beats. They recall the hymns that would have been intimately familiar to Dickinson from her childhood on. By far the most popular writer of these hymns was Isaac Watts, whose collections of hymns and other books could be found in every New England home. Opening Watts's *Divine Songs for Children* (1715), Dickinson would have encountered stanzas like this:

> Let dogs delight to bark and bite,
> For God hath made them so;
> Let bears and lions growl and fight,
> For 'tis their nature, too.

> But, children, you should never let
> Such angry passions rise;
> Your little hands were never made
> To tear each other's eyes.
> (from "Against Quarreling and Fighting")

Another perennially popular example of common measure is the hymn "Amazing Grace," which begins: "Amazing grace, how sweet the sound / That saved a wretch like me." But, although Dickinson's poems may superficially resemble sternly moralistic or sweetly consoling hymns, a closer look reveals that they are anything but:

> The Soul's superior instants
> Occur to Her alone,
> When friend and earth's occasion
> Have infinite withdrawn. (p. 275)

> Faith is a fine invention
> For gentlemen who see;
> But microscopes are prudent
> In an emergency! (p. 36)

Unfolding as predictably as a hymn, these two stanzas nevertheless show—with their preference for individuality over community, attention to detail over the "invention" of faith—how in Dickinson's crafty hands form is an occasion for cutting ironies, allowing her poems to enact an ongoing battle between received opinion and "superior instants." (The abrupt rhythm achieved by her characteristic use of dashes in place of expected punctuation also helps advance the battle; Dickinson's use of dashes may not always be evident in this edition, as discussed later in this essay.)

Dickinson's idiosyncratic use of rhyme adds even more tension to her deceptively hymn-like poems. "Tell all the Truth but tell it slant," she famously wrote (*The Complete Poems of Emily Dickinson*, edited by Thomas H. Johnson, poem 1129); and she practiced this wily doctrine in almost every poem:

> The heart asks pleasure first,
> And then, excuse from pain;
> And then, those little anodynes
> That deaden suffering;
>
> And then, to go to sleep;
> And then, if it should be
> The will of its Inquisitor,
> The liberty to die. (p. 10)

This wrenching little poem attains much of its power from Dickinson's use of "slant rhymes," or off-rhymes, like "pain–suffering" and "be–die," which don't allow the comfort that might come from exact rhymes and instead remind us of life's conflicts and near misses. Slant rhyme can also be a way to express the pleasure of messiness, the joy of not being able to "Tell all the Truth" once and for all:

> To tell the beauty would decrease,
> To state the Spell demean,
> There is a syllableless sea
> Of which it is the sign. (pp. 316–317)

Appropriately for a poem about how not "telling beauty" only increases beauty's strength, the near-rhymes "demean" and "sign" mirror the inexactness that Dickinson applauds. (The coinage "syllableless" is a good example of Dickinson's fondness for making up new words when the old ones are not adequate to her needs.)

Dickinson is as ardent a revisionist of syntax as she is of form, as is evident in the following single-stanza poem:

> Adventure most unto itself
> The Soul condemned to be;
> Attended by a Single Hound—
> Its own Identity. (p. 264)

Here, by reordering a statement that we might have expected to begin, "The Soul is condemned," Dickinson can start her poem with her true subject: the terror and the necessity of the soul's "Adventure." Similarly, by stripping the poem of verbs ("[is] condemned," "[It is] attended"), and by boldly capitalizing its final word, "Identity," she increases its starkness and strangeness. Isaac Watts would be appalled by such stylistic departures from tradition, but it is precisely these quirks that make Dickinson's poems so continually exciting.

Her liberties extend even further. Rather than begin her poems with elaborate contexts or settings, Dickinson plunges us right away into the pulsing heart of things. Her poems often start with a bold proclamation or definition that the rest of the poem explores: "Hope is the thing with feathers / That perches in the soul" (p. 22); "Heaven is what I cannot reach!" (p. 53); "Presentiment is that long shadow on the lawn" (p. 124). Other poems lead us straight into an extreme situation without warning:

> My life closed twice before its close;
>   It yet remains to see
> If Immortality unveil
>   A third event to me. (p. 56)

> I felt a cleavage in my mind
>   As if my brain had split;
> I tried to match it, seam by seam,
>   But could not make them fit. (p. 61)

> Wild nights! Wild nights!
> Were I with thee,
> Wild nights should be
> Our luxury! (p. 168)

Her endings can be just as abrupt. Whether a poem takes the form of a riddle, proverb, or narrative — for her genres are just as varied as her use of common measure is uniform — it often ends with a terrifying lack of closure. Two of her most well-known poems make this clear. In "Because I could not stop for Death," the speaker rides with Death in most leisurely fashion past children at play and the setting sun; but at the poem's end, time rushes suddenly forward, and the speaker looks back on the scene just described from the sudden vantage point of one who has been dead a long time:

> Since then 'tis centuries; but each
> Feels shorter than the day
> I first surmised the horses' heads
> Were toward eternity. (p. 201)

In "I heard a fly buzz when I died," Dickinson again assumes the role of a dead person and imagines the "stillness" of the scene around her, then brings the poem to a crashing halt with the following lines, horrifying for their utter absence of comfort or conclusion: "And then the windows failed, and then / I could not see to see" (p. 253).

Point of view in Dickinson's hands is an unstable thing, too.

The majority of her poems feature an "I" who tells stories, describes nature, or dissects belief (142 of them even begin with "I"), and her use of first-person perspective is every bit as innovative as is her handling of form, language, and structure. Writing to Higginson in July 1862, Dickinson remarked, "When I state myself, as the Representative of the Verse—it does not mean—me—but a supposed person" (*Selected Letters*, p. 176). Thus, in the two poems described above, Dickinson's narrators are not actual people who lived and died in a specific time and place, but emblematic figures whose deaths might just as well be ours. She also occasionally employs a "we" to narrate, as in the poem "Our journey had advanced" (p. 200).

Perhaps Dickinson's most radical departures from convention occur in her use of paradox to unsettle our most firmly held opinions and beliefs. As the critic Alfred Kazin writes, "She unsettles, most obviously, by not being easily locatable" (Kazin, "Wrecked, Solitary, Here: Dickinson's Room of Her Own," p. 164). To enter Dickinson's world is to step into a scary but electrifying funhouse where paradoxes serve like distorting mirrors to show us new ways of seeing just about everything: love, death, solitude, the soul. Throughout her work, opposites change places: Distance is nearness in disguise; absence is the most vital form of presence; aloneness is the greatest company. In several painful but illuminating poems, for example, she argues in favor of hunger and longing, maintaining that the lack that occasions desire makes the object of desire all the more precious:

> Success is counted sweetest
> By those who ne'er succeed.
> To comprehend a nectar
> Requires sorest need. (p. 6)

> I taste a liquor never brewed,
> From tankards scooped in pearl;
> Not all the vats upon the Rhine
> Yield such an alcohol! (p. 16)

> Delight becomes pictorial
> When viewed through pain,—
> More fair, because impossible
> That any gain. (pp. 29–30)

Elsewhere Dickinson uses paradox to destroy and reassemble our notions of other states of being, as when she writes, "Much madness is divinest sense / To a discerning eye" (p. 11), or asserts, "A death-blow is a life-blow to some" (p. 210), or describes just how deep still waters can run:

> The reticent volcano keeps
>   His never slumbering plan;
> Confided are his projects pink
>   To no precarious man. (p. 61)

But for all the paradoxes, a wonderfully direct and opinionated personality emerges from Dickinson's poems; the more of them we read, the more familiar we become with all her cranky, passionate likes and dislikes. Often she wears her disapproval on her sleeve, as in the following poem:

> What soft, cherubic creatures
>   These gentlewomen are!
> One would as soon assault a plush
>   Or violate a star.
>
> Such dimity convictions,
>   A horror so refined
> Of freckled human nature,
>   Of Deity ashamed,—
>
> It's such a common glory,
>   A fisherman's degree!
> Redemption, brittle lady,
>   Be so, ashamed of thee. (p. 72)

The poem's opening lines prepare us for a hymn of praise to these delicate ladies. But Dickinson's descriptions are double-edged: "Soft" connotes flimsy as well as feminine, and even though "cherubic" likens the women to angels, it also reveals their infantile, diminutive status. As the poem goes on, Dickinson's mocking scorn becomes more evident: The women are compared to "plush" — the filling of a sofa! — and their "star"-like nature may make them celestial, but it also puts them miserably out of touch with the real world. Their beliefs are as fragile as "dimity," a sheer cotton fabric; they are so "refined" that they cannot appreciate the rich complexity of "freckled human nature." As the poem reaches its close, Dickinson grows even harsher, calling the women "brittle" — a far cry from the first stanza's "soft" — and claiming that "Redemption" is "ashamed" of, and therefore unavailable to, these "creatures" in all their superficiality and passiveness.

Dickinson also disapproves of people who are incapable of feeling or showing emotions:

> A face devoid of love or grace,
> A hateful, hard, successful face,
>   A face with which a stone
> Would feel as thoroughly at ease
> As were they old acquaintances, —
>   First time together thrown. (p. 58)

If soft flimsiness is a fault in the previous poem, here it is stone-like hardness that Dickinson cannot abide; the face may be a conventionally "successful" one, but Dickinson is outraged by the idea that nothing deeper or richer lurks beneath it. Like the "gentlewomen" poem, with its references to "assaulting" and "violating," this poem contains hints of violence that reveal the depth of Dickinson's dislike: The last line conjures an almost wittily surreal image of the face and the stone being recklessly "thrown" at each other.

In two single-stanza poems, Dickinson expresses her strong distaste for still other personality types. She simply cannot understand how people can look at the world and not be fascinated by it:

> The Hills erect their purple heads,
> The Rivers lean to see—
> Yet Man has not, of all the throng,
> A curiosity. (p. 287)

She denounces people who don't know how to keep secrets:

> Candor, my tepid Friend,
> Come not to play with me!
> The Myrrhs and Mochas of the Mind
> Are its Iniquity. (p. 311)

While many appreciate directness, for Dickinson—who writes elsewhere in praise of indirection, claiming that "Success in Circuit lies" (*Complete Poems*, poem 1129)—directness creates a false sense of comfort, an overly perfumed "Myrrh" and a sickeningly sweet "Mocha."

In rich contrast to these poems, however, are moments in other poems when Dickinson lavishes praise on the types of people and behavior she does like. Pain, in her opinion, reveals people's depths more than any intrusive "candor":

> I like a look of agony
> Because I know it's true;
> Men do not sham convulsion,
> Nor simulate a throe.
>
> The eyes glaze once, and that is death.
> Impossible to feign
> The beads upon the forehead
> By homely anguish strung. (pp. 192–193)

Dickinson also heartily approves of those who are willing to put themselves in danger, since it puts them in touch with their own deepest "creases":

> Peril as a possession
> 'T is good to bear,

> Danger disintegrates satiety;
> There's Basis there
> Begets an awe,
> That searches Human Nature's creases
> As clean as Fire. (pp. 265–266)

She likes people who respect privacy:

> The suburbs of a secret
> A strategist should keep,
> Better than on a dream intrude
> To scrutinize the sleep. (pp. 271–272)

And she is utterly smitten with the transporting power of books, a love she reveals in poem after poem:

> There is no frigate like a book
>   To take us lands away,
> Nor any coursers like a page
>   Of prancing poetry.

> This traverse may the poorest take
>   Without oppress of toll;
> How frugal is the chariot
>   That bears a human soul! (pp. 57–58)

Even though Dickinson is one of the most difficult poets to interpret, she is also, as these poems reveal, one of the most refreshingly straightforward.

In Dickinson's work, apparent opposites—hunger and fulfillment, the self and God, death and life—turn out to have more in common than we'd thought. In her more explicitly religious poems, she violently overturns traditional Christian beliefs in order to create her own homespun theology. Despite her revisionary zeal, Dickinson never completely abandons her faith in God: "I know that he exists," she writes, "Somewhere, in silence" (p. 49). Rather, she is determined to explore new forms that God's "existence" might take. She is achingly up-front about her desire to know what God is really like:

> The Look of Thee, what is it like?
> Hast thou a hand or foot,
> Or mansion of Identity,
> And what is thy Pursuit? (p. 303)

But she also admits the possibility that we have invented the concept of life after death:

> Immortal is an ample word
>   When what we need is by,
> But when it leaves us for a time,
>   'T is a necessity. (p. 241)

She is capable of considerable anger about the rift between humans and God:

> Is Heaven a physician?
>   They say that He can heal;
> But medicine posthumous
>   Is unavailable. (p. 30)

Still, faced with this "unavailable" comfort, Dickinson responds not by giving up faith, but rather by constructing new versions of it. In several poems she asserts that the self's depths bring us as close to God as we can hope to come, and allow us a glimpse of what she calls "Finite Infinity" (p. 272):

> To be alive is power,
> Existence in itself,
> Without a further function,
> Omnipotence enough. (pp. 266–267)

Other poems locate divinity in nature:

The color on the cruising cloud,
  The interdicted ground,
Behind the hill, the house behind,—
  There Paradise is found! (p. 53)

In the name of the bee
And of the butterfly
And of the breeze, amen! (p. 110)

Whether looking inward or out her window, Dickinson radically replaces the traditional image of a distant, all-powerful God with a local divinity residing right by her side. Although "Some keep the Sabbath going to church," she writes, "I keep it staying at home. . . . / So instead of getting to heaven at last, / I'm going all along!" (p. 116). Dickinson never becomes complacent—she remains one of the greatest poets of loss—but she does find great solace in her bravely domestic cosmology:

Who has not found the heaven below
  Will fail of it above.
God's residence is next to mine,
  His furniture is love. (p. 58).

Because of her many poems about death—some of which happen to be among her most famous—Dickinson has been unfairly labeled a morbid poet. In fact, her interest in death makes perfect sense for a number of reasons. For one thing, Dickinson's subject matter is so varied that it would be stranger if she *didn't* write about death. Furthermore, as her biographer Cynthia Griffin Wolff has pointed out, Dickinson grew up in a culture highly preoccupied with death. Nineteenth-century children were taught to read with the *New England Primer*, which contained prayers that, as Wolff writes, "served to initiate even the youngest into an acknowledgment of death" (Wolff, *Emily Dickinson*, p. 69). Deaths from childbirth were extraordinarily common; New England gravestones frequently represented death with vivid and memorable icons; and deathbed vigils—so eerily described in "I heard a fly buzz" (p. 252)—were practically social events. Not surprisingly, this cultural saturation influenced Dickinson's poetry. This does not make her morbid; it merely shows how she transformed cultural preoccupations into poetic concerns. If Dickinson is obsessed with death, she is also capable of writing the most life-affirming of poems, as the following poem not included in this edition demonstrates:

> Did life's penurious length
> Italicize its sweetness,
> The men that daily live
> Would stand so deep in joy
> That it would clog the cogs
> Of that revolving reason
> Whose esoteric belt
> Protects our sanity. (*Complete Poems*, poem 1717)

Here, adding her bracing contribution to the *carpe diem* genre, Dickinson argues that an awareness of death can fill us with an intoxicating, almost crazy joy in being alive. It is one of the least morbid poems ever written.

The long, involved story of the posthumous fate of Dickinson's poems could fill its own volume. Only seven of her poems were published in her lifetime, five of them in the Springfield *Republican*. But after her death, her sister Lavinia discovered almost two thousand poems in her desk drawer, many written on scraps of paper or the back of grocery lists, others bound into what were later called "fascicles," or sewn paper booklets. Lavinia resolved to see them into print. Soon she had persuaded Mabel Loomis Todd and Thomas Higginson to help her edit the poems, and the three of them approached Robert Brothers, a publishing house in Boston. The first volume of *Poems* appeared in 1890 and became a bestseller. Already, however, the long history of modifying Dickinson's poems had begun, with some of her best and strangest lines omitted or changed, sentimental titles attached, rhymes regularized, and syntax standardized. Later editions, including *The Single Hound: Poems of a Lifetime* (1914), edited by Dickinson's niece Martha Dickinson Bianchi, also distorted the poems. In her acute short poem "Emily Dickinson," the contemporary British poet Wendy Cope wryly comments on this unfortunate trend:

> Higgledy-piggledy
> Emily Dickinson
> Liked to use dashes
> Instead of full stops.
>
> Nowadays, faced with such
> Idiosyncrasy,
> Critics and editors
> Send for the cops.
> (Cope, *Making Cocoa for Kingsley Amis*, p. 23)

Finally, in 1955, Thomas H. Johnson's *The Poems of Emily Dickinson* offered readers access to all of Dickinson's poems, arranged in estimated chronological order and with her idiosyncrasies — slant rhymes, dashes, capitals — intact. Johnson's restored text went a long way toward undoing the follies of earlier editors. (To take just one example, Todd and Higginson had changed "Because I could not stop for Death" (p. 200) so that the line "Cornice — in the Ground" read "The cornice but a mound," thereby reducing an eerily sinking grave to a simple pile of dirt.)

For a long while (until the publication in 1999 of an edition of the poems by R. W. Franklin), most readers, scholars, and teachers regarded Johnson's edition as the authoritative one. But for some, it did not go far enough. The critics Sharon Cameron and Susan Howe, for example, argue that the variant words Dickinson often included at the bottom of a manuscript page should be read as essential parts of the poems; among Dickinson's myriad innovations, they claim, is a new approach to poetics in which writers and readers need not always choose one word and meanings can proliferate in fruitful mayhem. (Cameron, *Choosing Not Choosing: Dickinson's Fascicles*, and Howe, *My Emily Dickinson*). Others have complained that the fascicles should be treated as separate volumes; or that Johnson's division of most of the poems into quatrains is too sweeping and Dickinson's stanza divisions are more varied than he allowed. In the original manuscript, for example, the first words of the poem "A Narrow Fellow in the Grass" (p. 96) are on two lines, with "the Grass" set as a separate line against the left margin; Johnson argues that this was due to lack of writing space, but others suggest a more deliberate experimentation with line breaks on Dickinson's part.

It should be noted that this edition arranges Dickinson's poems by theme, and regularizes her punctuation and capitalization; readers eager for a version of the poems closer to the manuscripts should seek out Johnson's edition, as well as the stimulating criticism of Cameron, Howe, and others.

In a poem not included in this edition, Dickinson wrote about the posthumous fate of poets:

> The Poets light but Lamps—
> Themselves—go out—
> The wicks they stimulate—
> If vital Light
>
> Inhere as do the Suns—
> Each Age a Lens
> Disseminating their
> Circumference—(*Complete Poems*, poem 883)

Crudely paraphrased, the poem asserts that after poets die, they are interpreted—if they are "vital" enough—in different ways by different people. This has certainly been the case with Dickinson, who has influenced later writers in an astonishing variety of ways.

Hart Crane's sonnet "To Emily Dickinson," though it overlooks her wit and range, tenderly invokes a "sweet, dead Silencer":

> You who desired so much—in vain to ask—
> Yet fed your hunger like an endless task,
> Dared dignify the labor, bless the quest—
> Achieved that stillness ultimately best.
> (Crane, *The Poems of Hart Crane*, p. 128)

Here and elsewhere, Crane's obsessive use of dashes shows that Dickinson's ghost was never far from his side. Archibald MacLeish claimed, somewhat condescendingly, "Most of us are half in love with this girl" (in Bogan, *Emily Dickinson: Three Views*, p. 20). William Carlos Williams remarked in an interview,

> She was an independent spirit. . . . She did her best to get away from too strict an interpretation. And she didn't want to be confirmed to rhyme or reason. . . . And she followed the American idiom. . . . She was a wild girl. She chafed against restraint. But she speaks the spoken language, the idiom, which would be deformed by Oxford English. . . . She was a real good guy (Williams, *Poets at Work: The Paris Review Interviews*, p. 169).

Elizabeth Bishop, though she admitted that "I still hate the oh-the-pain-of-it-all poems," noted, "I admire many others" (Kalstone, *Becoming a Poet*, p. 132).

Confessional poetry, with its harsh excavations of the self's deepest places, would not be as rich without Dickinson's example. Robert Frost, though seldom classed as a confessional poet, wrote several poems in which exploration of his "Desert Places" leads him to a terrifying inner antagonist, a "blanker whiteness" (Frost, *The Poetry of Robert Frost*, p. 296) that recalls both Dickinson's customary dress color and her observations: "Pain has an element of blank" (p. 16) and "One need not be a chamber to be haunted" (p. 224). Finding depths within oneself, of course, can be cause for celebration as well as fear, a fact of which Wallace Stevens seems acutely aware in these lines from "Tea at the Palaz of Hoon":

> Out of my mind the golden ointment rained,
> And my ears made the blowing hymns they heard.
> I was myself the compass of that sea:
>
> I was the world in which I walked, and what I saw
> Or heard or felt came not but from myself;
> And there I found myself more truly and more strange.
> (Stevens, *The Collected Poems*, p. 65)

Here, as often happens in Dickinson's work, the human and the divine change places, and the mind's capacity is found to be equal or superior to God's.

Several later poets, like Dickinson before them, make death a character: Anne Sexton titled one of her poems "For Mr. Death Who Stands with His Door Open," and Sylvia Plath's "Death & Co." personifies not one but *two* Deaths. (There are also numerous moments in the work of both poets when they imagine their own deaths.) And the popular poet Billy Collins cheerfully profanes Dickinson's woman-in-white mystique in "Taking Off Emily Dickinson's Clothes," describing how

> I could plainly hear her inhale
> when I undid the very top
> hook-and-eye fastener of her corset
>
> and I could hear her sigh when finally it was unloosed,
> the way some readers sigh when they realize
> that Hope has feathers,
> that reason is a plank,
> that life is a loaded gun
> that looks right at you with a yellow eye.
> (Collins, *Picnic, Lightning*, p. 75)

Adrienne Rich, in several striking poems, presents a feisty and determined Dickinson. In the fourth section of "Snapshots of a Daughter-in-Law," she portrays her

> Reading while waiting
> for the iron to heat,
> writing, *My Life had stood—a Loaded Gun—*
> in that Amherst pantry while the jellies boil and scum,
> or, more often,
> iron-eyed and beaked and purposed as a bird,
> dusting everything on the whatnot every day of life.
> (Rich, *The Fact of a Doorframe*, p. 18)

And in "The Spirit of Place," Rich angrily describes the Emily Dickinson Industry's invasion of her home:

> In Emily Dickinson's house in Amherst
> cocktails are served   the scholars
> gather in celebration
> their pious or clinical legends
> festoon the walls like imitations
> of period patterns.
> (Rich, *The Fact of a Doorframe*, p. 184)

But despite "The remnants pawed   the relics / the cult assembled in the bedroom," the scholars do not get the last word, for "you whose teeth were set on edge by churches / resist your shrine / escape." Rich vows that her relationship to Dickinson will be a very different one in which "with the hands of a daughter I would cover you / from all intrusion   even my own   / saying   rest to your ghost" (Rich, *The Fact of a Doorframe*, pp. 184–185).

Dickinson's widespread influence can perhaps best be seen in poets who are in most ways nothing like her. e.e. cummings, as formally explosive as Dickinson was—at least superficially—conservative, begins one poem in this way:

> my father moved through dooms of love
> through sames of am through haves of give,
> singing each morning out of each night
> my father moved through depths of height
> (*e.e. cummings: Complete Poems 1904–1962*, p. 520)

cummings's "dooms of love," "sames of am," and "haves of give" recall Dickinson's peculiar use of the genitive case in a poem in which she describes heaven as "The House of Supposition" that "Skirts the Acres of Perhaps" (*Complete Poems*, poem 696). In addition, the paradoxes of the third and fourth lines of cummings's stanza—"each morning out of each night" and "depths of height"—resemble Dickinson's characteristic trait, discussed earlier, of translating big into small, life into death, and—in the case of poem 696, riches into poverty: "The Wealth I had—contented me—/ If 'twas a meaner size—".

Dickinson has even made her way into fiction. Judith Farr's 1996 novel *I Never Came to You in White* offers a fictionalized biography of Dickinson. And in A. S. Byatt's 1990 novel *Possession: A Romance*—a double love story in which two modern academics investigate the secret love affair of two Victorian poets, Randolph Henry Ash and Christabel LaMotte—Dickinson is the model for the female heroine. At the beginning of the novel, Byatt provides a list of some of the more silly-sounding articles critics have written about her heroine:

> They wrote on "Arachne's Broken Woof: Art as Discarded Spinning in the Poems of LaMotte." Or "Melusina and the Daemonic Double: Good Mother, Bad Serpent." "A Docile Rage: Christabel LaMotte's Ambivalent Domesticity" (Byatt, *Possession: A Romance*, p. 43).

But before long, these limited views of LaMotte give way to a much more rich and complex one, mostly because Byatt lets the poet speak for her eccentric, resourceful self, as in this letter:

> I have chosen a Way—dear Friend—I must hold to it. Think of me if you will as the Lady of Shalott—with a Narrower Wisdom— who chooses not the Gulp of Outside Air and the chilly river-journey deathwards—but who chooses to watch diligently the bright colours of her Web—to ply an industrious shuttle—to make—something—to close the Shutters and the Peephole too— (Byatt, p. 205).

Dickinson's influence can be felt everywhere. Writers are in her thrall; every year the Poetry Society of America offers an award "for a poem inspired by Dickinson"; the 2002 Modern Language Association featured several panels on her work; she even has her own International Society. As Dickinson herself predicted, her light may have gone out, but the lenses of later ages keep reflecting and refracting it in all sorts of inventive and unexpected ways. The intense eyes of the young woman in the photograph will keep peering into ours for a very long time.

Rachel Wetzsteon received her doctorate in English from Columbia University in 1999 and is Assistant Professor of English at William Paterson University. She has published two books of poems, *The Other Stars* and *Home and Away,* and has received various awards for her poetry. She currently lives in New York City.

THE COLLECTED POEMS
OF EMILY DICKINSON

PART ONE

LIFE

THIS is my letter to the world,
  That never wrote to me, —
The simple news that Nature told,
  With tender majesty.

Her message is committed
  To hands I cannot see;
For love of her, sweet countrymen,
  Judge tenderly of me!

I

SUCCESS is counted sweetest
By those who ne'er succeed.
To comprehend a nectar
Requires sorest need.

Not one of all the purple host
Who took the flag to-day
Can tell the definition,
So clear, of victory,

As he, defeated, dying,
On whose forbidden ear
The distant strains of triumph
Break, agonized and clear.

II

OUR share of night to bear,
Our share of morning,
Our blank in bliss to fill,
Our blank in scorning.

Here a star, and there a star,
Some lose their way.
Here a mist, and there a mist,
Afterwards — day!

6

III

SOUL, wilt thou toss again?
By just such a hazard
Hundreds have lost, indeed,
But tens have won an all.

Angels' breathless ballot
Lingers to record thee;
Imps in eager caucus
Raffle for my soul.

IV

'T is so much joy! 'T is so much joy!
If I should fail, what poverty!
And yet, as poor as I
Have ventured all upon a throw;
Have gained! Yes! Hesitated so
This side the victory!

Life is but life, and death but death!
Bliss is but bliss, and breath but breath!
And if, indeed, I fail,
At least to know the worst is sweet.
Defeat means nothing but defeat,
No drearier can prevail!

And if I gain, — oh, gun at sea,
Oh, bells that in the steeples be,
At first repeat it slow!
For heaven is a different thing
Conjectured, and waked sudden in,
And might o'erwhelm me so!

V

GLEE! the great storm is over!
Four have recovered the land;
Forty gone down together
Into the boiling sand.

Ring, for the scant salvation!
Toll, for the bonnie* souls, —
Neighbor and friend and bridegroom,
Spinning upon the shoals!

How they will tell the shipwreck
When winter shakes the door,
Till the children ask, "But the forty?
Did they come back no more?"

Then a silence suffuses the story,
And a softness the teller's eye;
And the children no further question,
And only the waves reply.

VI

IF I can stop one heart from breaking,
I shall not live in vain;
If I can ease one life the aching,
Or cool one pain,
Or help one fainting robin
Unto his nest again,
I shall not live in vain.

---

*Attractive, pretty (Scottish).

VII

WITHIN my reach!
I could have touched!
I might have chanced that way!
Soft sauntered through the village,
Sauntered as soft away!
So unsuspected violets
Within the fields lie low,
Too late for striving fingers
That passed, an hour ago.

VIII

A wounded deer leaps highest,
I've heard the hunter tell;
'T is but the ecstasy of death,
And then the brake* is still.

The smitten rock that gushes,
The trampled steel that springs:
A cheek is always redder
Just where the hectic¹ stings!

Mirth is the mail of anguish,
In which it caution arm,
Lest anybody spy the blood
And "You're hurt" exclaim!

---

*Rough, overgrown land.
†Fluctuating, persistent fever, such as accompanies tuberculosis.

IX

THE heart asks pleasure first,
And then, excuse from pain;
And then, those little anodynes*
That deaden suffering;

And then, to go to sleep;
And then, if it should be
The will of its Inquisitor,
The liberty to die.

X

A precious, mouldering pleasure 't is
To meet an antique book,
In just the dress his century wore;
A privilege, I think,

His venerable hand to take,
And warming in our own,
A passage back, or two, to make
To times when he was young.

His quaint opinions to inspect,
His knowledge to unfold
On what concerns our mutual mind,
The literature of old;

What interested scholars most,
What competitions ran

*Things that soothe or eliminate pain.

When Plato was a certainty,
And Sophocles a man;

When Sappho* was a living girl,
And Beatrice† wore
The gown that Dante deified.
Facts, centuries before,

He traverses familiar,
As one should come to town
And tell you all your dreams were true:
He lived where dreams were born.

His presence is enchantment,
You beg him not to go;
Old volumes shake their vellum‡ heads
And tantalize, just so.

XI

MUCH madness is divinest sense
To a discerning eye;
Much sense the starkest madness.
'T is the majority
In this, as all, prevails.
Assent, and you are sane;
Demur, — you're straightway dangerous,
And handled with a chain.

---

*Greek lyric poet (c.600 B.C.) of Lesbos, whose work survives only in fragments.
†Beatrice Portinari, Dante's muse, who appears in his epic poem *The Divine Comedy* (1308–1321).
‡Fine-grained calfskin, lambskin, or kidskin used for the pages and bindings of books.

XII

I asked no other thing,
No other was denied.
I offered Being for it;
The mighty merchant smiled.

Brazil? He twirled a button,
Without a glance my way:
"But, madam, is there nothing else
That we can show to-day?"

XIII

THE soul selects her own society,
Then shuts the door;
On her divine majority
Obtrude no more.

Unmoved, she notes the chariot's pausing
At her low gate;
Unmoved, an emperor is kneeling
Upon her mat.

I've known her from an ample nation
Choose one;
Then close the valves of her attention
Like stone.

XIV

SOME things that fly there be, —
Birds, hours, the bumble-bee:
Of these no elegy.

Some things that stay there be, —
Grief, hills, eternity:
Nor this behooveth* me.

There are, that resting, rise.
Can I expound the skies?
How still the riddle lies!

XV

I know some lonely houses off the road
A robber'd like the look of, —
Wooden barred,
And windows hanging low,
Inviting to
A portico,

Where two could creep:
One hand the tools,
The other peep
To make sure all's asleep.
Old-fashioned eyes,
Not easy to surprise!

How orderly the kitchen'd look by night,
With just a clock, —
But they could gag the tick,
And mice won't bark;
And so the walls don't tell,
None will.

A pair of spectacles ajar just stir —
An almanac's aware.
Was it the mat winked,

*Is necessary or proper for.

Or a nervous star?
The moon slides down the stair
To see who's there.

There's plunder,—where?
Tankard,* or spoon,
Earring, or stone,
A watch, some ancient brooch
To match the grandmamma,
Staid sleeping there.

Day rattles, too,
Stealth's slow;
The sun has got as far
As the third sycamore.
Screams chanticleer,†
"Who's there?"

And echoes, trains away,
Sneer—"Where?"
While the old couple, just astir,
Think that the sunrise left the door ajar!

XVI

To fight aloud is very brave,
But gallanter, I know,
Who charge within the bosom,
The cavalry of woe.

Who win, and nations do not see,
Who fall, and none observe,

---

*Tall, single-handled drinking vessel.
†Rooster.

Whose dying eyes no country
Regards with patriot love.

We trust, in plumed procession,
For such the angels go,
Rank after rank, with even feet
And uniforms of snow.

XVII

WHEN night is almost done,
And sunrise grows so near
That we can touch the spaces,
It's time to smooth the hair

And get the dimples ready,
And wonder we could care
For that old faded midnight
That frightened but an hour.

XVIII

READ, sweet, how others strove,
'Till we are stouter;
What they renounced,
Till we are less afraid;
How many times they bore
The faithful witness,
Till we are helped,
As if a kingdom cared!

Read then of faith
That shone above the fagot;*
Clear strains of hymn
The river could not drown;
Brave names of men
And celestial women,
Passed out of record
Into renown!

XIX

PAIN has an element of blank;
It cannot recollect
When it began, or if there were
A day when it was not.

It has no future but itself,
Its infinite realms contain
Its past, enlightened to perceive
New periods of pain.

XX

I taste a liquor never brewed,
From tankards scooped in pearl;
Not all the vats upon the Rhine
Yield such an alcohol!

Inebriate of air am I,
And debauchee of dew,

*Bundle of sticks or branches bound together.

Reeling, through endless summer days,
From inns of molten blue.

When landlords turn the drunken bee
Out of the foxglove's* door,
When butterflies renounce their drams,†
I shall but drink the more!

Till seraphs† swing their snowy hats,
And saints to windows run,
To see the little tippler
Leaning against the sun!

XXI

HE ate and drank the precious words,
His spirit grew robust;
He knew no more that he was poor,
Nor that his frame was dust.
He danced along the dingy days,
And this bequest of wings
Was but a book. What liberty
A loosened spirit brings!

XXII

I had no time to hate, because
The grave would hinder me,

*Plant with speckled white, purplish, or yellow tubular flowers.
†Small portions.
‡Angels of the highest order.

And life was not so ample I
Could finish enmity.

Nor had I time to love; but since
Some industry must be,
The little toil of love, I thought,
Was large enough for me.

XXIII

'T was such a little, little boat
That toddled down the bay!
'T was such a gallant, gallant sea
That beckoned it away!

'T was such a greedy, greedy wave
That licked it from the coast:
Nor ever guessed the stately sails
My little craft was lost!

XXIV

WHETHER my bark* went down at sea,
Whether she met with gales,
Whether to isles enchanted
She bent her docile sails;

By what mystic mooring
She is held to-day, —
This is the errand of the eye
Out upon the bay.

---

*Small sailing ship.

XXV

BELSHAZZAR* had a letter, —
He never had but one;
Belshazzar's correspondent
Concluded and begun
In that immortal copy
The conscience of us all
Can read without its glasses
On revelation's wall.

XXVI

THE brain within its groove
Runs evenly and true;
But let a splinter swerve,
'T were easier for you
To put the water back
When floods have slit the hills,
And scooped a turnpike for themselves,
And blotted out the mills!

XXVII

I'M nobody! Who are you?
Are you nobody, too?
Then there's a pair of us — don't tell!
They'd banish us, you know.

---

*Last king of Babylonia (c.540 B.C.); in the Bible, he was warned of his death by mysterious writing that appeared on the wall of his palace (see Daniel 5).

How dreary to be somebody!
How public, like a frog
To tell your name the livelong day
To an admiring bog!

XXVIII

I bring an unaccustomed wine
To lips long parching, next to mine,
And summon them to drink.

Crackling with fever, they essay;*
I turn my brimming eyes away,
And come next hour to look.

The hands still hug the tardy glass;
The lips I would have cooled, alas!
Are so superfluous cold,

I would as soon attempt to warm
The bosoms where the frost has lain
Ages beneath the mould.

Some other thirsty there may be
To whom this would have pointed me
Had it remained to speak.

And so I always bear the cup
If, haply, mine may be the drop
Some pilgrim thirst to slake, —

---

*Try.

If, haply, any say to me,
"Unto the little, unto me,"*
When I at last awake.

XXIX

THE nearest dream recedes, unrealized.
        The heaven we chase
        Like the June bee
        Before the school-boy
        Invites the race;
        Stoops to an easy clover —
Dips — evades — teases — deploys;
        Then to the royal clouds
        Lifts his light pinnace†
        Heedless of the boy
Staring, bewildered, at the mocking sky.

        Homesick for steadfast honey,
        Ah! the bee flies not
That brews that rare variety.

XXX

WE play at paste,
Till qualified for pearl,
Then drop the paste,
And deem ourself a fool.

---

*Reference to the Bible, Matthew 19:14: "But Jesus said, Suffer little children, and forbid them not, to come unto me" (King James Version; henceforth KJV).
†Small sailing ship.

The shapes, though, were similar,
And our new hands
Learned gem-tactics
Practising sands.

XXXI

I found the phrase to every thought
I ever had, but one;
And that defies me, — as a hand
Did try to chalk the sun

To races nurtured in the dark; —
How would your own begin?
Can blaze be done in cochineal,
Or noon in mazarin?*

XXXII

HOPE is the thing with feathers
That perches in the soul,
And sings the tune without the words,
And never stops at all,

And sweetest in the gale is heard;
And sore must be the storm
That could abash the little bird
That kept so many warm.

---

*Cochineal is a red dye made from female cochineal insects; mazarin is a deep purplish blue.

I've heard it in the chillest land,
And on the strangest sea;
Yet, never, in extremity,
It asked a crumb of me.

XXXIII

DARE you see a soul at the white heat?
    Then crouch within the door.
Red is the fire's common tint;
    But when the vivid ore

Has sated flame's conditions,
    Its quivering substance plays
Without a color but the light
    Of unanointed blaze.

Least village boasts its blacksmith,
    Whose anvil's even din
Stands symbol for the finer forge
    That soundless tugs within,

Refining these impatient ores
    With hammer and with blaze,
Until the designated light
    Repudiate the forge.

XXXIV

WHO never lost, are unprepared
A coronet to find;

Who never thirsted, flagons*
And cooling tamarind.†

Who never climbed the weary league—
Can such a foot explore
The purple territories
On Pizarro's‡ shore?

How many legions overcome?
The emperor will say.
How many colors taken
On Revolution Day?

How many bullets bearest?
The royal scar hast thou?
Angels, write "Promoted"
On this soldier's brow!

XXXV

I can wade grief,
Whole pools of it,—
I'm used to that.
But the least push of joy
Breaks up my feet,
And I tip—drunken.
Let no pebble smile,
'T was the new liquor,—
That was all!

---

*Large vessels for holding wine or other drinks.
†Fruit of a tropical Asian tree, used to make cold drinks.
‡Francisco Pizarro (c.1475–1541), Spanish explorer and conqueror of Peru.

Power is only pain,
Stranded, through discipline,
Till weights will hang.
Give balm to giants,
And they'll wilt, like men.
Give Himmaleh, — *
They'll carry him!

XXXVI

I never hear the word "escape"
Without a quicker blood,
A sudden expectation,
A flying attitude.

I never hear of prisons broad
By soldiers battered down,
But I tug childish at my bars, —
Only to fail again!

XXXVII

FOR each ecstatic instant
We must an anguish pay
In keen and quivering ratio
To the ecstasy.

For each beloved hour
Sharp pittances of years,

---

*The reference is to the Himalaya, a range in south-central Asia.

Bitter contested farthings*
And coffers heaped with tears.

XXXVIII

THROUGH the straight pass of suffering
The martyrs even trod,
Their feet upon temptation,
Their faces upon God.

A stately, shriven company;
Convulsion playing round,
Harmless as streaks of meteor
Upon a planet's bound.

Their faith the everlasting troth;†
Their expectation fair;
The needle to the north degree
Wades so, through polar air.

XXXIX

I meant to have but modest needs,
Such as content, and heaven;
Within my income these could lie,
And life and I keep even.

But since the last included both,
It would suffice my prayer

---

*Coins formerly used in Great Britain, worth about one-fourth of a penny.
†Pledge of fidelity; betrothal.

But just for one to stipulate,
And grace would grant the pair.

And so, upon this wise I prayed, —
Great Spirit, give to me
A heaven not so large as yours,
But large enough for me.

A smile suffused Jehovah's* face;
The cherubim† withdrew;
Grave saints stole out to look at me,
And showed their dimples, too.

I left the place with all my might, —
My prayer away I threw;
The quiet ages picked it up,
And Judgment twinkled, too,

That one so honest be extant
As take the tale for true
That "Whatsoever you shall ask,
Itself be given you."

But I, grown shrewder, scan the skies
With a suspicious air, —
As children, swindled for the first,
All swindlers be, infer.

XI.

THE thought beneath so slight a film
Is more distinctly seen, —

---

*God's; Jehovah, a variation of Yahweh, is a name the ancient Hebrews used for
the deity.
†Angels of the second-highest order.

As laces just reveal the surge,
Or mists the Apennine.*

XLI

THE soul unto itself
Is an imperial friend, —
Or the most agonizing spy
An enemy could send.

Secure against its own,
No treason it can fear;
Itself its sovereign, of itself
The soul should stand in awe.

XLII

SURGEONS must be very careful
When they take the knife!
Underneath their fine incisions
Stirs the culprit, — Life!

XLIII

I like to see it lap the miles,
And lick the valleys up,

---

*The Apennines are a mountain chain in Italy.

And stop to feed itself at tanks;
And then, prodigious, step

Around a pile of mountains,
And, supercilious, peer
In shanties by the sides of roads;
And then a quarry pare

To fit its sides, and crawl between,
Complaining all the while
In horrid, hooting stanza;
Then chase itself down hill

And neigh like Boanerges;*
Then, punctual as a star,
Stop—docile and omnipotent—
At its own stable door.

XLIV

THE show is not the show,
But they that go.
Menagerie to me
My neighbor be.
Fair play—
Both went to see.

XLV

DELIGHT becomes pictorial
When viewed through pain,—

---

*Meaning a loud preacher or orator; in the Bible (Mark 3:14–17) Boanerges, "sons of thunder," is the surname Jesus gave to his disciples James and John.

More fair, because impossible
That any gain.

The mountain at a given distance
In amber lies;
Approached, the amber flits a little, —
And that's the skies!

XLVI

A thought went up my mind to-day
That I have had before,
But did not finish, — some way back,
I could not fix the year,

Nor where it went, nor why it came
The second time to me,
Nor definitely what it was,
Have I the art to say.

But somewhere in my soul, I know
I've met the thing before;
It just reminded me — 't was all —
And came my way no more.

XLVII

Is Heaven a physician?
    They say that He can heal;
But medicine posthumous
    Is unavailable.

Is Heaven an exchequer?*
    They speak of what we owe;
But that negotiation
    I'm not a party to.

XLVIII

THOUGH I get home how late, how late!
So I get home, 't will compensate.
Better will be the ecstasy
That they have done expecting me,
When, night descending, dumb and dark,
They hear my unexpected knock.
Transporting must the moment be,
Brewed from decades of agony!

To think just how the fire will burn,
Just how long-cheated eyes will turn
To wonder what myself will say,
And what itself will say to me,
Beguiles the centuries of way!

XLIX

A poor torn heart, a tattered heart,
That sat it down to rest,
Nor noticed that the ebbing day
Flowed silver to the west,
Nor noticed night did soft descend

---

*British governmental department charged with the collection and management of the national revenue.

Nor constellation burn,
Intent upon the vision
Of latitudes unknown.

The angels, happening that way,
This dusty heart espied;
Tenderly took it up from toil
And carried it to God.
There,—sandals for the barefoot;
There,—gathered from the gales,
Do the blue havens by the hand
Lead the wandering sails.

L

I should have been too glad, I see,
Too lifted for the scant degree
   Of life's penurious round;
My little circuit would have shamed
This new circumference, have blamed
   The homelier time behind.

I should have been too saved, I see,
Too rescued; fear too dim to me
   That I could spell the prayer
I knew so perfect yesterday,—
That scalding one, "Sabachthani,"*
   Recited fluent here.

Earth would have been too much, I see,
And heaven not enough for me;

---

*At his Crucifixion, Christ cried down from the cross: "Eli, Eli, lama sabach-
thani?" The phrase means, "My God, my God, why hast thou forsaken me?"
(Aramaic; see the Bible, Matthew 27:46, KJV).

I should have had the joy
Without the fear to justify,—
The palm without the Calvary;*
    So, Saviour, crucify.

Defeat whets victory, they say;
The reefs in old Gethsemane†
    Endear the shore beyond.
'T is beggars banquets best define;
'T is thirsting vitalizes wine,—
    Faith faints to understand.

LI

It tossed and tossed,—
A little brig‡ I knew,—
O'ertook by blast,
It spun and spun,
And groped delirious, for morn.

It slipped and slipped,
As one that drunken stepped;
Its white foot tripped,
Then dropped from sight.

Ah, brig, good-night
To crew and you;

---

*"Palm" refers to the palms the populace spread in his path to welcome Jesus when he entered Jerusalem a week before his Crucifixion; Palm Sunday (the Sunday before Easter) commemorates that event. Calvary is a hill outside the city where Jesus was crucified.
†Garden outside Jerusalem where Jesus was betrayed (see the Bible, Matthew 26: 36–50).
‡Two-masted sailing ship.

The ocean's heart too smooth, too blue,
To break for you.

LII

VICTORY comes late,
And is held low to freezing lips
Too rapt with frost
To take it.
How sweet it would have tasted,
Just a drop!
Was God so economical?
His table's spread too high for us
Unless we dine on tip-toe.
Crumbs fit such little mouths,
Cherries suit robins;
The eagle's golden breakfast
Strangles them.
God keeps his oath to sparrows,
Who of little love
Know how to starve!

LIII

GOD gave a loaf to every bird,
But just a crumb to me;
I dare not eat it, though I starve, —
My poignant luxury
To own it, touch it, prove the feat
That made the pellet mine, —
Too happy in my sparrow chance
For ampler coveting.

It might be famine all around,
I could not miss an ear,
Such plenty smiles upon my board,
My garner* shows so fair.
I wonder how the rich may feel, —
An Indiaman — an Earl?
I deem that I with but a crumb
Am sovereign of them all.

LIV

EXPERIMENT to me
Is every one I meet.
If it contain a kernel?
The figure of a nut

Presents upon a tree,
Equally plausibly;
But meat within is requisite,
To squirrels and to me.

LV

My country need not change her gown,
Her triple suit as sweet
As when 't was cut at Lexington,†
And first pronounced "a fit."

---

*Granary.
†Town in northeastern Massachusetts; site of a battle fought on April 19, 1775, that marked the start of the American Revolution.

Great Britain disapproves "the stars";
Disparagement discreet, —
There's something in their attitude
That taunts her bayonet.

LVI

FAITH is a fine invention
For gentlemen who see;
But microscopes are prudent
In an emergency!

LVII

EXCEPT the heaven had come so near,
So seemed to choose my door,
The distance would not haunt me so;
I had not hoped before.

But just to hear the grace depart
I never thought to see,
Afflicts me with a double loss;
'T is lost, and lost to me.

LVIII

PORTRAITS are to daily faces
As an evening west

To a fine, pedantic sunshine
In a satin vest.

LIX

I took my power in my hand
And went against the world;
'T was not so much as David* had,
But I was twice as bold.

I aimed my pebble, but myself
Was all the one that fell.
Was it Goliath was too large,
Or only I too small?

LX

A shady friend for torrid days
Is easier to find
Than one of higher temperature
For frigid hour of mind.

The vane a little to the east
Scares muslin souls away;
If broadcloth breasts are firmer
Than those of organdy,†

---

*In the Bible (1 Samuel 17), the young shepherd David, who became king of Judah and Israel, used a slingshot and stones to kill Goliath, champion of the Philistines.

†Muslin is a plain-woven cotton fabric; broadcloth a densely textured woolen fabric; and organdy a stiff, transparent fabric of cotton or silk.

Who is to blame? The weaver?
Ah! the bewildering thread!
The tapestries of paradise
So notelessly are made!

LXI

EACH life converges to some centre
Expressed or still;
Exists in every human nature
A goal,

Admitted scarcely to itself, it may be,
Too fair
For credibility's temerity
To dare.

Adored with caution, as a brittle heaven,
To reach
Were hopeless as the rainbow's raiment*
To touch,

Yet persevered toward, surer for the distance;
How high
Unto the saints' slow diligence
The sky!

Ungained, it may be, by a life's low venture,
But then,
Eternity enables the endeavoring
Again.

---

*Clothing.

LXII

BEFORE I got my eye put out,
I liked as well to see
As other creatures that have eyes,
And know no other way.

But were it told to me, to-day,
That I might have the sky
For mine, I tell you that my heart
Would split, for size of me.

The meadows mine, the mountains mine,—
All forests, stintless* stars,
As much of noon as I could take
Between my finite eyes.

The motions of the dipping birds,
The lightning's jointed road,
For mine to look at when I liked,—
The news would strike me dead!

So, safer, guess, with just my soul
Upon the window-pane
Where other creatures put their eyes,
Incautious of the sun.

LXIII

TALK with prudence to a beggar
Of "Potosi"† and the mines!

---

*Meaning without cease; a good example of Dickinson's habit of coining words.
†City in south-central Bolivia, founded after silver was discovered there in 1545.

Reverently to the hungry
Of your viands* and your wines!

Cautious, hint to any captive
You have passed enfranchised feet!
Anecdotes of air in dungeons
Have sometimes proved deadly sweet!

LXIV

HE preached upon "breadth" till it argued him
        narrow, —
The broad are too broad to define;
And of "truth" until it proclaimed him a liar, —
The truth never flaunted a sign.

Simplicity fled from his counterfeit presence
As gold the pyrites† would shun.
What confusion would cover the innocent Jesus
To meet so enabled a man!

LXV

GOOD night! which put the candle out?
A jealous zephyr,‡ not a doubt.
    Ah! friend, you little knew
How long at that celestial wick

---

*Food; delicious dishes.
†Metallic sulfide minerals, most commonly, gold-colored pyrite.
‡Gentle breeze.

The angels labored diligent;
　　Extinguished, now, for you!

It might have been the lighthouse spark
Some sailor, rowing in the dark,
　　Had importuned to see!
It might have been the waning lamp
That lit the drummer from the camp
　　To purer reveille!*

LXVI

WHEN I hoped I feared,
Since I hoped I dared;
Everywhere alone
As a church remain;
Spectre cannot harm,
Serpent cannot charm;
He deposes doom,
Who hath suffered him.

LXVII

A deed knocks first at thought,
And then it knocks at will.
That is the manufacturing spot,
And will at home and well.

It then goes out an act,
Or is entombed so still

---

*Wake-up call, especially from a bugle.

That only to the ear of God
Its doom is audible.

LXVIII

MINE enemy is growing old, —
I have at last revenge.
The palate of the hate departs;
If any would avenge, —

Let him be quick, the viand flits,
It is a faded meat.
Anger as soon as fed is dead;
'T is starving makes it fat.

LXIX

REMORSE is memory awake,
Her companies astir, —
A presence of departed acts
At window and at door.

Its past set down before the soul,
And lighted with a match,
Perusal to facilitate
Of its condensed despatch.

Remorse is cureless, — the disease
Not even God can heal;
For 't is His institution, —
The complement of hell.

LXX

THE body grows outside, —
The more convenient way, —
That if the spirit like to hide,
Its temple stands alway

Ajar, secure, inviting;
It never did betray
The soul that asked its shelter
In timid honesty.

LXXI

UNDUE significance a starving man attaches
To food
Far off; he sighs, and therefore hopeless,
And therefore good.

Partaken, it relieves indeed, but proves us
That spices fly
In the receipt. It was the distance
Was savory.

LXXII

HEART not so heavy as mine,
Wending late home,
As it passed my window
Whistled itself a tune, —

A careless snatch, a ballad,
A ditty of the street;
Yet to my irritated ear
An anodyne so sweet,

It was as if a bobolink,*
Sauntering this way,
Carolled and mused and carolled,
Then bubbled slow away.

It was as if a chirping brook
Upon a toilsome way
Set bleeding feet to minuets†
Without the knowing why.

To-morrow, night will come again,
Weary, perhaps, and sore.
Ah, bugle, by my window,
I pray you stroll once more!

LXXIII

I many times thought peace had come,
When peace was far away;
As wrecked men deem they sight the land
At centre of the sea,

And struggle slacker, but to prove,
As hopelessly as I,
How many the fictitious shores
Before the harbor lie.

---

*American migratory songbird.
†Slow, stately dances that originated in seventeenth-century France.

LXXIV

UNTO my books so good to turn
Far ends of tired days;
It half endears the abstinence,
And pain is missed in praise.

As flavors cheer retarded guests
With banquetings to be,
So spices stimulate the time
Till my small library.

It may be wilderness without,
Far feet of failing men,
But holiday excludes the night,
And it is bells within.

I thank these kinsmen of the shelf;
Their countenances bland
Enamour in prospective,*
And satisfy, obtained.

LXXV

THIS merit hath the worst, —
It cannot be again.
When Fate hath taunted last
And thrown her furthest stone,

The maimed may pause and breathe,
And glance securely round.

---

*In the future; likely to come about.

The deer invites no longer
Than it eludes the hound.

LXXVI

I had been hungry all the years;
My noon had come, to dine;
I, trembling, drew the table near,
And touched the curious wine.

'T was this on tables I had seen,
When turning, hungry, lone,
I looked in windows, for the wealth
I could not hope to own.

I did not know the ample bread,
'T was so unlike the crumb
The birds and I had often shared
In Nature's dining-room.

The plenty hurt me, 't was so new, —
Myself felt ill and odd,
As berry of a mountain bush
Transplanted to the road.

Nor was I hungry; so I found
That hunger was a way
Of persons outside windows,
The entering takes away.

LXXVII

I gained it so,
By climbing slow,

By catching at the twigs that grow
Between the bliss and me.
    It hung so high,
    As well the sky
    Attempt by strategy.

I said I gained it, —
    This was all.
Look, how I clutch it,
    Lest it fall,
And I a pauper go;
Unfitted by an instant's grace
For the contented beggar's face
I wore an hour ago.

LXXVIII

To learn the transport by the pain,
As blind men learn the sun;
To die of thirst, suspecting
That brooks in meadows run,

To stay the homesick, homesick feet
Upon a foreign shore
Haunted by native lands, the while,
And blue, beloved air —

This is the sovereign anguish,
This, the signal woe!
These are the patient laureates*
Whose voices, trained below,

*Those honored or awarded prizes for great achievements.

Ascend in ceaseless carol,
Inaudible, indeed,
To us, the duller scholars
Of the mysterious bard!

LXXIX

I years had been from home,
And now, before the door,
I dared not open, lest a face
I never saw before

Stare vacant into mine
And ask my business there.
My business,—just a life I left,
Was such still dwelling there?

I fumbled at my nerve,
I scanned the windows near;
The silence like an ocean rolled,
And broke against my ear.

I laughed a wooden laugh
That I could fear a door,
Who danger and the dead had faced,
But never quaked before.

I fitted to the latch
My hand, with trembling care,
Lest back the awful door should spring,
And leave me standing there.

I moved my fingers off
As cautiously as glass,

And held my ears, and like a thief
Fled gasping from the house.

LXXX

PRAYER is the little implement
Through which men reach
Where presence is denied them.
They fling their speech

By means of it in God's ear;
If then He hear,
This sums the apparatus
Comprised in prayer.

LXXXI

I know that he exists
Somewhere, in silence.
He has hid his rare life
From our gross eyes.

'T is an instant's play,
'T is a fond ambush,
Just to make bliss
Earn her own surprise!

But should the play
Prove piercing earnest,
Should the glee glaze
In death's stiff stare,

Would not the fun
Look too expensive?
Would not the jest
Have crawled too far?

LXXXII

MUSICIANS wrestle everywhere:
All day, among the crowded air,
    I hear the silver strife;
And—waking long before the dawn—
Such transport breaks upon the town
    I think it that "new life!"

It is not bird, it has no nest;
Nor band, in brass and scarlet dressed,
    Nor tambourine, nor man;
It is not hymn from pulpit read,—
The morning stars the treble led
    On time's first afternoon!

Some say it is the spheres at play!
Some say that bright majority
    Of vanished dames and men!
Some think it service in the place
Where we, with late, celestial face,
    Please God, shall ascertain!

LXXXIII

JUST lost when I was saved!
Just felt the world go by!

Just girt* me for the onset with eternity,
When breath blew back,
And on the other side
I heard recede the disappointed tide!

Therefore, as one returned, I feel,
Odd secrets of the line to tell!
Some sailor, skirting foreign shores,
Some pale reporter from the awful doors
Before the seal!

Next time, to stay!
Next time, the things to see
By ear unheard,
Unscrutinized by eye.

Next time, to tarry,
While the ages steal, —
Slow tramp the centuries,
And the cycles wheel.

LXXXIV

'T is little I could care for pearls
    Who own the ample sea;
Or brooches, when the Emperor
    With rubies pelteth me;

Or gold, who am the Prince of Mines;
    Or diamonds, when I see
A diadem† to fit a dome
    Continual crowning me.

---

*Strapped or encircled, as with a belt or band.
†Crown.

LXXXV

SUPERIORITY to fate
    Is difficult to learn.
'T is not conferred by any,
    But possible to earn

A pittance at a time,
    Until, to her surprise,
The soul with strict economy
    Subsists till Paradise.

LXXXVI

HOPE is a subtle glutton;
    He feeds upon the fair;
And yet, inspected closely,
    What abstinence is there!

His is the halcyon table
    That never seats but one,
And whatsoever is consumed
    The same amounts remain.

LXXXVII

FORBIDDEN fruit a flavor has
    That lawful orchards mocks;
How luscious lies the pea within
    The pod that Duty locks!

LXXXVIII

HEAVEN is what I cannot reach!
    The apple on the tree,
Provided it do hopeless hang,
    That "heaven" is, to me.

The color on the cruising cloud,
    The interdicted* ground
Behind the hill, the house behind, —
    There Paradise is found!

LXXXIX

A word is dead
When it is said,
    Some say.
I say it just
Begins to live
    That day.

XC

To venerate the simple days
Which lead the seasons by,
Needs but to remember
    That from you or me
They may take the trifle
    Termed mortality!

---

*Forbidden.

To invest existence with a stately air,
Needs but to remember
    That the acorn there
Is the egg of forests
    For the upper air!

XCI

IT's such a little thing to weep,
So short a thing to sigh;
And yet by trades the size of these
    We men and women die!

XCII

DROWNING is not so pitiful
    As the attempt to rise.
Three times, 't is said, a sinking man
    Comes up to face the skies,
And then declines forever
    To that abhorred abode
Where hope and he part company, —
    For he is grasped of God.
The Maker's cordial visage,
    However good to see,
Is shunned, we must admit it,
    Like an adversity.

XCIII

How still the bells in steeples stand,
    Till, swollen with the sky,

They leap upon their silver feet
In frantic melody!

XCIV

If the foolish call them "flowers,"
    Need the wiser tell?
If the savants "classify" them,
    It is just as well!

Those who read the *Revelations*
    Must not criticise
Those who read the same edition
    With beclouded eyes!

Could we stand with that old Moses
    Canaan denied, —
Scan, like him, the stately landscape
    On the other side, —

Doubtless we should deem superfluous
    Many sciences
Not pursued by learned angels
    In scholastic skies!

Low amid that glad *Belles lettres**
    Grant that we may stand,
Stars, amid profound Galaxies,
    At that grand "Right hand"!

---

*Light literary or intellectual writings (French).

XCV

Could mortal lip divine
      The undeveloped freight
Of a delivered syllable,
      'T would crumble with the weight.

XCVI

My life closed twice before its close;
      It yet remains to see
If Immortality unveil
      A third event to me,

So huge, so hopeless to conceive,
      As these that twice befell.
Parting is all we know of heaven,
      And all we need of hell.

XCVII

We never know how high we are
      Till we are called to rise;
And then, if we are true to plan,
      Our statures touch the skies.

The heroism we recite
      Would be a daily thing,

Did not ourselves the cubits* warp
    For fear to be a king.

XCVIII

WHILE I was fearing it, it came,
    But came with less of fear,
Because that fearing it so long
    Had almost made it dear.
There is a fitting a dismay,
    A fitting a despair.
'T is harder knowing it is due,
    Than knowing it is here.
The trying on the utmost,
    The morning it is new,
Is terribler than wearing it
    A whole existence through.

XCIX

THERE is no frigate† like a book
    To take us lands away,
Nor any coursers† like a page
    Of prancing poetry.

This traverse may the poorest take
    Without oppress of toll;

---

*Ancient units of linear measure.
†High-speed sailing vessel.
‡Swift horses.

How frugal is the chariot
That bears a human soul!

C

Who has not found the heaven below
    Will fail of it above.
God's residence is next to mine,
    His furniture is love.

CI

A face devoid of love or grace,
A hateful, hard, successful face,
    A face with which a stone
Would feel as thoroughly at ease
As were they old acquaintances, —
    First time together thrown.

CII

I had a guinea* golden;
    I lost it in the sand,
And though the sum was simple,
    And pounds were in the land,
Still had it such a value
    Unto my frugal eye,

*Gold coin issued in England from 1663 to 1813, worth one pound, one shilling.

That when I could not find it
    I sat me down to sigh.

I had a crimson robin
    Who sang full many a day,
But when the woods were painted
    He, too, did fly away.
Time brought me other robins, —
    Their ballads were the same, —
Still for my missing troubadour*
    I kept the "house at hame."†

I had a star in heaven;
    One Pleiad‡ was its name,
And when I was not heeding
    It wandered from the same.
And though the skies are crowded,
    And all the night ashine,
I do not care about it,
    Since none of them are mine.

My story has a moral:
    I have a missing friend, —
Pleiad its name, and robin,
    And guinea in the sand, —
And when this mournful ditty,
    Accompanied with tear,
Shall meet the eye of traitor
    In country far from here,
Grant that repentance solemn
    May seize upon his mind,

*In medieval Europe, a lyric poet who wrote and performed songs about courtly love.
†Home (Scottish).
‡One of the Pleiades, a star cluster named for the daughters of Atlas in Greek mythology.

And he no consolation
    Beneath the sun may find.

CIII

FROM all the jails the boys and girls
    Ecstatically leap, —
Beloved, only afternoon
    That prison doesn't keep.

They storm the earth and stun the air,
    A mob of solid bliss.
Alas! that frowns could lie in wait
    For such a foe as this!

CIV

FEW get enough, — enough is one;
    To that ethereal throng
Have not each one of us the right
    To stealthily belong?

CV

UPON the gallows hung a wretch,
    Too sullied for the hell
    To which the law entitled him.
    As nature's curtain fell
The one who bore him tottered in,

For this was woman's son.
" 'T was all I had," she stricken gasped;
    Oh, what a livid boon!

CVI

I felt a cleavage in my mind
    As if my brain had split;
I tried to match it, seam by seam,
    But could not make them fit.

The thought behind I strove to join
    Unto the thought before,
But sequence ravelled out of reach
    Like balls upon a floor.

CVII

THE reticent volcano keeps
    His never slumbering plan;
Confided are his projects pink
    To no precarious man.

If nature will not tell the tale
    Jehovah told to her,
Can human nature not survive
    Without a listener?

Admonished by her buckled lips
    Let every babbler be.
The only secret people keep
    Is Immortality.

CVIII

IF recollecting were forgetting,
    Then I remember not;
And if forgetting, recollecting,
    How near I had forgot!
And if to miss were merry,
    And if to mourn were gay,
How very blithe the fingers
    That gathered these to-day!

CIX

THE farthest thunder that I heard
    Was nearer than the sky,
And rumbles still, though torrid noons
    Have lain their missiles by.
The lightning that preceded it
    Struck no one but myself,
But I would not exchange the bolt
    For all the rest of life.
Indebtedness to oxygen
    The chemist may repay,
But not the obligation
    To electricity.
It founds the homes and decks the days,
    And every clamor bright
Is but the gleam concomitant*
    Of that waylaying light.
The thought is quiet as a flake, —
    A crash without a sound;

---

*Accompanying.

How life's reverberation
    Its explanation found!

CX

On the bleakness of my lot
    Bloom I strove to raise.
Late, my acre of a rock
    Yielded grape and maize.

Soil of flint if steadfast tilled
    Will reward the hand;
Seed of palm by Lybian sun
    Fructified in sand.

CXI

A door just opened on a street—
    I, lost, was passing by—
An instant's width of warmth disclosed,
    And wealth, and company,

The door as sudden shut, and I,
    I, lost, was passing by,—
Lost doubly, but by contrast most,
    Enlightening misery.

CXII

Are friends delight or pain?
Could bounty but remain
    Riches were good.

But if they only stay
Bolder to fly away,
    Riches are sad.

CXIII

Ashes denote that fire was;
    Respect the grayest pile
For the departed creature's sake
    That hovered there awhile.

Fire exists the first in light,
    And then consolidates, —
Only the chemist can disclose
    Into what carbonates.*

CXIV

Fate slew him, but he did not drop;
    She felled — he did not fall —
Impaled him on her fiercest stakes —
    He neutralized them all.

She stung him, sapped his firm advance,
    But, when her worst was done,
And he, unmoved, regarded her,
    Acknowledged him a man.

---

*Salts or esters of carbonic acid, which releases carbon dioxide.

CXV

FINITE to fail, but infinite to venture.
    For the one ship that struts the shore
Many's the gallant, overwhelmed creature
    Nodding in navies nevermore.

CXVI

I measure every grief I meet
    With analytic eyes;
I wonder if it weighs like mine,
    Or has an easier size.

I wonder if they bore it long,
    Or did it just begin?
I could not tell the date of mine,
    It feels so old a pain.

I wonder if it hurts to live,
    And if they have to try,
And whether, could they choose between,
    They would not rather die.

I wonder if when years have piled—
    Some thousands—on the cause
Of early hurt, if such a lapse
    Could give them any pause;

Or would they go on aching still
    Through centuries above,
Enlightened to a larger pain
    By contrast with the love.

The grieved are many, I am told;
    The reason deeper lies,—
Death is but one and comes but once,
    And only nails the eyes.

There's grief of want, and grief of cold,—
    A sort they call "despair";
There's banishment from native eyes,
    In sight of native air.

And though I may not guess the kind
    Correctly, yet to me
A piercing comfort it affords
    In passing Calvary,

To note the fashions of the cross,
    Of those that stand alone,
Still fascinated to presume
    That some are like my own.

CXVII

I have a king who does not speak;
So, wondering, thro' the hours meek
    I trudge the day away,—
Half glad when it is night and sleep,
If, haply, thro' a dream to peep
    In parlors shut by day.

And if I do, when morning comes,
It is as if a hundred drums
    Did round my pillow roll,
And shouts fill all my childish sky,
And bells keep saying "victory"
    From steeples in my soul!

And if I don't, the little Bird
Within the Orchard is not heard,
 And I omit to pray,
"Father, thy will be done"* to-day,
For my will goes the other way,
 And it were perjury!

CXVIII

It dropped so low in my regard
 I heard it hit the ground,
And go to pieces on the stones
 At bottom of my mind;

Yet blamed the fate that fractured, less
 Than I reviled myself
For entertaining plated wares
 Upon my silver shelf.

CXIX

To lose one's faith surpasses
 The loss of an estate,
Because estates can be
 Replenished, — faith cannot.

Inherited with life,
 Belief but once can be;
Annihilate a single clause,
 And Being's beggary.

---

*Dickinson is quoting from the Lord's Prayer.

CXX

I had a daily bliss
    I half indifferent viewed,
Till sudden I perceived it stir, —
    It grew as I pursued,

Till when, around a crag,
    It wasted from my sight,
Enlarged beyond my utmost scope,
    I learned its sweetness right.

CXXI

I worked for chaff, and earning wheat
    Was haughty and betrayed.
What right had fields to arbitrate
    In matters ratified?

I tasted wheat, — and hated chaff,
    And thanked the ample friend;
Wisdom is more becoming viewed
    At distance than at hand.

CXXII

Life, and Death, and Giants
Such as these, are still.
Minor apparatus, hopper* of the mill,

---

*Funnel-shaped device used to feed grain into a mill.

Beetle at the candle,
  Or a fife's* small fame,
Maintain by accident
That they proclaim.

CXXIII

OUR lives are Swiss, —
So still, so cool,
  Till, some odd afternoon,
The Alps neglect their curtains,
  And we look farther on.

Italy stands the other side,
  While, like a guard between,
The solemn Alps,
The siren Alps,
  Forever intervene!

CXXIV

REMEMBRANCE has a rear and front, —
  'T is something like a house;
It has a garret† also
  For refuse and the mouse,

Besides, the deepest cellar
  That ever mason hewed;‡

---

*Small flute.
†Room or unfinished part of a house just under the roof.
‡Cut with blows of a heavy instrument.

Look to it, by its fathoms
    Ourselves be not pursued.

CXXV

To hang our head ostensibly,
    And subsequent to find
That such was not the posture
    Of our immortal mind,

Affords the sly presumption
    That, in so dense a fuzz,
You, too, take cobweb attitudes
    Upon a plane of gauze!

CXXVI

THE brain is wider than the sky,
    For, put them side by side,
The one the other will include
    With ease, and you beside.

The brain is deeper than the sea,
    For, hold them, blue to blue,
The one the other will absorb,
    As sponges, buckets do.

The brain is just the weight of God,
    For, lift them, pound for pound,
And they will differ, if they do,
    As syllable from sound.

CXXVII

THE bone that has no marrow;
    What ultimate for that?
It is not fit for table,
    For beggar, or for cat.

A bone has obligations,
    A being has the same;
A marrowless assembly
    Is culpabler than shame.

But how shall finished creatures
    A function fresh obtain? —
Old Nicodemus'* phantom
    Confronting us again!

CXXVIII

THE past is such a curious creature,
    To look her in the face
A transport may reward us,
    Or a disgrace.

Unarmed if any meet her,
    I charge him, fly!
Her rusty ammunition
    Might yet reply!

---

*In the Bible, Nicodemus was a Pharisee and a ruler of the Jews. Jesus said, "Except a man be born again, he cannot see the kingdom of God." Nicodemus asked Jesus, "How can a man be born when he is old?" (John 3:3–4, KJV).

CXXIX

To help our bleaker parts
    Salubrious hours are given,
Which if they do not fit for earth
    Drill silently for heaven.

CXXX

WHAT soft, cherubic creatures
    These gentlewomen are!
One would as soon assault a plush
    Or violate a star.

Such dimity* convictions,
    A horror so refined
Of freckled human nature,
    Of Deity ashamed, —

It's such a common glory,
    A fisherman's degree!
Redemption, brittle lady,
    Be so, ashamed of thee.

CXXXI

WHO never wanted, — maddest joy
    Remains to him unknown;

---

*Dimity is a sheer cotton fabric of plain weave in checks or stripes.

The banquet of abstemiousness*
    Surpasses that of wine.

Within its hope, though yet ungrasped
    Desire's perfect goal,
No nearer, lest reality
    Should disenthrall thy soul.

CXXXII

It might be easier
    To fail with land in sight,
Than gain my blue peninsula
    To perish of delight.

CXXXIII

You cannot put a fire out;
    A thing that can ignite
Can go, itself, without a fan
    Upon the slowest night.

You cannot fold a flood
    And put it in a drawer, —
Because the winds would find it out,
    And tell your cedar floor.

---

*Restraint.

CXXXIV

A modest lot, a fame *petite*,
A brief campaign of sting and sweet
    Is plenty! Is enough!
A sailor's business is the shore,
    A soldier's — balls. Who asketh more
Must seek the neighboring life!

CXXXV

Is bliss, then, such abyss
I must not put my foot amiss
For fear I spoil my shoe?

I'd rather suit my foot
Than save my boot,
For yet to buy another pair
Is possible
At any fair.

But bliss is sold just once;
The patent lost
None buy it any more.

CXXXVI

I stepped from plank to plank
    So slow and cautiously;
The stars about my head I felt,
    About my feet the sea.

I knew not but the next
  Would be my final inch, —
This gave me that precarious gait
  Some call experience.

CXXXVII

ONE day is there of the series
  Termed Thanksgiving day,
Celebrated part at table,
  Part in memory.

Neither patriarch nor pussy,
  I dissect the play;
Seems it, to my hooded thinking,
  Reflex holiday.

Had there been no sharp subtraction
  From the early sum,
Not an acre or a caption
  Where was once a room,

Not a mention, whose small pebble
  Wrinkled any bay, —
Unto such, were such assembly,
  'T were Thanksgiving day.

CXXXVIII

SOFTENED by Time's consummate plush,
  How sleek the woe appears

That threatened childhood's citadel
    And undermined the years!

Bisected now by bleaker griefs,
    We envy the despair
That devastated childhood's realm,
    So easy to repair.

PART TWO

NATURE

My nosegays are for captives;
    Dim, long-expectant eyes,
Fingers denied the plucking,
    Patient till paradise.

To such, if they should whisper
    Of morning and the moor,
They bear no other errand,
    And I, no other prayer.

I

NATURE, the gentlest mother,
Impatient of no child,
The feeblest or the waywardest, —
Her admonition mild

In forest and the hill
By traveller is heard,
Restraining rampant squirrel
Or too impetuous bird.

How fair her conversation,
A summer afternoon, —
Her household, her assembly;
And when the sun goes down

Her voice among the aisles
Incites the timid prayer
Of the minutest cricket,
The most unworthy flower.

When all the children sleep
She turns as long away
As will suffice to light her lamps;
Then, bending from the sky,

With infinite affection
And infiniter care,
Her golden finger on her lip,
Wills silence everywhere.

II

WILL there really be a morning?
Is there such a thing as day?
Could I see it from the mountains
If I were as tall as they?

Has it feet like water-lilies?
Has it feathers like a bird?
Is it brought from famous countries
Of which I have never heard?

Oh, some scholar! Oh, some sailor!
Oh, some wise man from the skies!
Please to tell a little pilgrim
Where the place called morning lies!

III

AT half-past three a single bird
Unto a silent sky
Propounded but a single term
Of cautious melody.

At half-past four, experiment
Had subjugated test,
And lo! her silver principle
Supplanted all the rest.

At half-past seven, element
Nor implement was seen,
And place was where the presence was,
Circumference between.

IV

THE day came slow, till five o'clock,
Then sprang before the hills
Like hindered rubies, or the light
A sudden musket spills.

The purple could not keep the east,
The sunrise shook from fold,
Like breadths of topaz, packed a night,
The lady just unrolled.

The happy winds their timbrels* took;
The birds, in docile rows,
Arranged themselves around their prince
(The wind is prince of those).

The orchard sparkled like a Jew,—
How mighty 't was, to stay
A guest in this stupendous place,
The parlor of the day!

V

THE sun just touched the morning;
The morning, happy thing,
Supposed that he had come to dwell,
And life would be all spring.

She felt herself supremer,—
A raised, ethereal thing;

---

*Small hand drums or tambourines.

Henceforth for her what holiday!
Meanwhile, her wheeling king

Trailed slow along the orchards
His haughty, spangled hems,
Leaving a new necessity, —
The want of diadems!

The morning fluttered, staggered,
Felt feebly for her crown, —
Her unanointed forehead
Henceforth her only one.

VI

THE robin is the one
That interrupts the morn
With hurried, few, express reports
When March is scarcely on.

The robin is the one
That overflows the noon
With her cherubic quantity,
An April but begun.

The robin is the one
That speechless from her nest
Submits that home and certainty
And sanctity are best.

VII

FROM cocoon forth a butterfly
As lady from her door

Emerged—a summer afternoon—
Repairing everywhere,

Without design, that I could trace,
Except to stray abroad
On miscellaneous enterprise
The clovers understood.

Her pretty parasol was seen
Contracting in a field
Where men made hay, then struggling hard
With an opposing cloud,

Where parties, phantom as herself,
To Nowhere seemed to go
In purposeless circumference,
As 't were a tropic show.

And notwithstanding bee that worked,
And flower that zealous blew,
This audience of idleness
Disdained them, from the sky,

Till sundown crept, a steady tide,
And men that made the hay,
And afternoon, and butterfly,
Extinguished in its sea.

VIII

BEFORE you thought of spring,
Except as a surmise,
You see, God bless his suddenness,
A fellow in the skies
Of independent hues,

A little weather-worn,
Inspiriting habiliments*
Of indigo and brown.

With specimens of song,
As if for you to choose,
Discretion in the interval,
With gay delays he goes
To some superior tree
Without a single leaf,
And shouts for joy to nobody
But his seraphic self!

IX

AN altered look about the hills;
A Tyrian† light the village fills;
A wider sunrise in the dawn;
A deeper twilight on the lawn;
A print of a vermilion‡ foot;
A purple finger on the slope;
A flippant fly upon the pane;
A spider at his trade again;

An added strut in chanticleer;
A flower expected everywhere;
An axe shrill singing in the woods;
Fern-odors on untravelled roads, —
All this, and more I cannot tell,
A furtive look you know as well,

*Clothing.
†Tyre was an ancient Phoenician city on the eastern Mediterranean Sea in what is today southern Lebanon.
‡Vivid reddish orange.

And Nicodemus' mystery
Receives its annual reply.

X

"WHOSE are the little beds," I asked,
"Which in the valleys lie?"
Some shook their heads, and others smiled,
And no one made reply.

"Perhaps they did not hear," I said;
"I will inquire again.
Whose are the beds, the tiny beds
So thick upon the plain?"

" 'T is daisy in the shortest;
A little farther on,
Nearest the door to wake the first,
Little leontodon.*

" 'T is iris, sir, and aster,
Anemone and bell,
Batschia in the blanket red,
And chubby daffodil."

Meanwhile at many cradles
Her busy foot she plied,
Humming the quaintest lullaby
That ever rocked a child.

---

*Old name for a late-flowering aster. Other plants mentioned include: anemone,
a type of buttercup; batschia, the old name for a plant with delicate blue flowers;
epigea, a trailing evergreen shrub; and rhodora, an azalea with rose-purple flowers.

"Hush! Epigea wakens!
The crocus stirs her lids,
Rhodora's cheek is crimson, —
She's dreaming of the woods."

Then, turning from them, reverent,
"Their bed-time 't is," she said;
"The bumble-bees will wake them
When April woods are red."

XI

PIGMY seraphs gone astray,
Velvet people from Vevay,*
Belles from some lost summer day,
Bees' exclusive coterie.
Paris could not lay the fold
Belted down with emerald;
Venice could not show a cheek
Of a tint so lustrous meek.
Never such an ambuscade†
As of brier and leaf displayed
For my little damask‡ maid.
I had rather wear her grace
Than an earl's distinguished face;
I had rather dwell like her
Than be Duke of Exeter,§
Royalty enough for me
To subdue the bumble-bee!

---

*Town in Switzerland.
†Ambush.
‡Lustrous fabric made with flat patterns in a satin weave.
§Borough of southwestern England.

XII

To hear an oriole sing
May be a common thing,
Or only a divine.

It is not of the bird
Who sings the same, unheard,
As unto crowd.

The fashion of the ear
Attireth that it hear
In dun* or fair.

So whether it be rune,†
Or whether it be none,
Is of within;

The "tune is in the tree,"
The sceptic showeth me;
"No, sir! In thee!"

XIII

ONE of the ones that Midas touched,
Who failed to touch us all,
Was that confiding prodigal,
The blissful oriole.

---

*Marked by dullness and drabness.
†Mystical poem or incantation.

So drunk, he disavows it
With badinage* divine;
So dazzling, we mistake him
For an alighting mine.

A pleader, a dissembler,
An epicure, a thief,—
Betimes an oratorio,†
An ecstasy in chief;

The Jesuit of orchards,
He cheats as he enchants
Of an entire attar‡
For his decamping wants.

The splendor of a Burmah,§
The meteor of birds,
Departing like a pageant
Of ballads and of bards.

I never thought that Jason** sought
For any golden fleece;
But then I am a rural man,
With thoughts that make for peace.

But if there were a Jason,
Tradition suffer me
Behold his lost emolument††
Upon the apple-tree.

---

*Playful repartee, banter.
†Lengthy, usually religious, choral work.
‡Fragrant oil.
§Burma, now known as Myanmar, is a country in southeastern Asia.
**Mythological hero and leader of the Argonauts, who went in search of the Golden Fleece.
††Payment, compensation.

XIV

I dreaded that first robin so,
But he is mastered now,
And I'm accustomed to him grown, —
He hurts a little, though.

I thought if I could only live
Till that first shout got by,
Not all pianos in the woods
Had power to mangle me.

I dared not meet the daffodils,
For fear their yellow gown
Would pierce me with a fashion
So foreign to my own.

I wished the grass would hurry,
So when 't was time to see,
He'd be too tall, the tallest one
Could stretch to look at me.

I could not bear the bees should come,
I wished they'd stay away
In those dim countries where they go:
What word had they for me?

They're here, though; not a creature failed,
No blossom stayed away
In gentle deference to me,
The Queen of Calvary.

Each one salutes me as he goes,
And I my childish plumes
Lift, in bereaved acknowledgment
Of their unthinking drums.

XV

A route of evanescence
With a revolving wheel;
A resonance of emerald,
A rush of cochineal;
And every blossom on the bush
Adjusts its tumbled head,—
The mail from Tunis,* probably,
An easy morning's ride.

XVI

THE skies can't keep their secret!
They tell it to the hills—
The hills just tell the orchards—
And they the daffodils!

A bird, by chance, that goes that way
Soft overheard the whole.
If I should bribe the little bird,
Who knows but she would tell?

I think I won't, however,
It's finer not to know;
If summer were an axiom,
What sorcery had snow?

So keep your secret, Father!
I would not, if I could,

---

*Capital of Tunisia, a country in northern Africa.

Know what the sapphire fellows do,
In your new-fashioned world!

XVII

WHO robbed the woods,
The trusting woods?
The unsuspecting trees
Brought out their burrs and mosses
His fantasy to please.
He scanned their trinkets, curious,
He grasped, he bore away.
What will the solemn hemlock,
What will the fir-tree say?

XVIII

Two butterflies went out at noon
And waltzed above a stream.
Then stepped straight through the firmament
And rested on a beam;

And then together bore away
Upon a shining sea, —
Though never yet, in any port,
Their coming mentioned be.

If spoken by the distant bird,
If met in ether sea
By frigate or by merchantman,
Report was not to me.

XIX

I started early, took my dog,
And visited the sea;
The mermaids in the basement
Came out to look at me,

And frigates in the upper floor
Extended hempen* hands,
Presuming me to be a mouse
Aground, upon the sands.

But no man moved me till the tide
Went past my simple shoe,
And past my apron and my belt,
And past my bodice too,

And made as he would eat me up
As wholly as a dew
Upon a dandelion's sleeve —
And then I started too.

And he — he followed close behind;
I felt his silver heel
Upon my ankle, — then my shoes
Would overflow with pearl.

Until we met the solid town,
No man he seemed to know;
And bowing with a mighty look
At me, the sea withdrew.

---

*Composed of hemp, a tough, fibrous plant used to make rope.

XX

ARCTURUS* is his other name,—
I'd rather call him star!
It's so unkind of science
To go and interfere!

I pull a flower from the woods,—
A monster with a glass
Computes the stamens in a breath,
And has her in a class.

Whereas I took the butterfly
Aforetime in my hat,
He sits erect in cabinets,
The clover-bells forgot.

What once was heaven, is zenith now.
Where I proposed to go
When time's brief masquerade was done,
Is mapped, and charted too!

What if the poles should frisk about
And stand upon their heads!
I hope I'm ready for the worst,
Whatever prank betides!†

Perhaps the kingdom of Heaven's changed!
I hope the children there
Won't be new-fashioned when I come,
And laugh at me, and stare!

---

*Fourth-brightest star in the sky and the brightest in the constellation Boötes.
†Happens.

I hope the father in the skies
Will lift his little girl, —
Old-fashioned, naughty, everything, —
Over the stile* of pearl!

XXI

An awful tempest mashed the air,
The clouds were gaunt and few;
A black, as of a spectre's cloak,
Hid heaven and earth from view.

The creatures chuckled on the roofs
And whistled in the air,
And shook their fists and gnashed their teeth,
And swung their frenzied hair.

The morning lit, the birds arose;
The monster's faded eyes
Turned slowly to his native coast,
And peace was Paradise!

XXII

An everywhere of silver,
With ropes of sand
To keep it from effacing
The track called land.

---

*Step or steps for passing over a fence or wall.

XXIII

A bird came down the walk:
He did not know I saw;
He bit an angle-worm* in halves
And ate the fellow, raw.

And then he drank a dew
From a convenient grass,
And then hopped sidewise to the wall
To let a beetle pass.

He glanced with rapid eyes
That hurried all abroad, —
They looked like frightened beads, I thought
He stirred his velvet head

Like one in danger; cautious,
I offered him a crumb,
And he unrolled his feathers
And rowed him softer home

Than oars divide the ocean,
Too silver for a seam,
Or butterflies, off banks of noon,
Leap, plashless,† as they swim.

XXIV

A narrow fellow in the grass
Occasionally rides;

---

*Earthworm.
†Without a splash.

You may have met him,—did you not?
His notice sudden is.

The grass divides as with a comb,
A spotted shaft is seen;
And then it closes at your feet
And opens further on.

He likes a boggy acre,
A floor too cool for corn.
Yet when a child, and barefoot,
I more than once, at morn,

Have passed, I thought, a whip-lash
Unbraiding in the sun,—
When, stooping to secure it,
It wrinkled, and was gone.

Several of nature's people
I know, and they know me;
I feel for them a transport
Of cordiality;

But never met this fellow,
Attended or alone,
Without a tighter breathing,
And zero at the bone.

XXV

THE mushroom is the elf of plants,
At evening it is not;

At morning in a truffled* hut
It stops upon a spot

As if it tarried always;
And yet its whole career
Is shorter than a snake's delay,
And fleeter than a tare.†

'T is vegetation's juggler,
The germ of alibi;
Doth like a bubble antedate,
And like a bubble hie.

I feel as if the grass were pleased
To have it intermit;
The surreptitious scion
Of summer's circumspect.

Had nature any outcast face,
Could she a son contemn,
Had nature an Iscariot,‡
That mushroom, — it is him.

XXVI

THERE came a wind like a bugle;
It quivered through the grass,
And a green chill upon the heat
So ominous did pass
We barred the windows and the doors
As from an emerald ghost;

---

*Covered with truffles (fungi that are considered a delicacy).
†Weedy plant, especially the common vetch.
‡Judas Iscariot, who betrayed Jesus (see the Bible, Matthew 26:14–16).

The doom's electric moccason
That very instant passed.
On a strange mob of panting trees,
And fences fled away,
And rivers where the houses ran
The living looked that day.
The bell within the steeple wild
The flying tidings whirled.
How much can come
And much can go,
And yet abide the world!

XXVII

A spider sewed at night
Without a light
Upon an arc of white.
If ruff it was of dame
Or shroud of gnome,
Himself, himself inform.
Of immortality
His strategy
Was physiognomy.*

XXVIII

I know a place where summer strives
With such a practised frost,
She each year leads her daisies back,
Recording briefly, "Lost."

---

*Art of discovering character from outward appearance.

But when the south wind stirs the pools
And struggles in the lanes,
Her heart misgives her for her vow,
And she pours soft refrains

Into the lap of adamant,*
And spices, and the dew,
That stiffens quietly to quartz,
Upon her amber shoe.

XXIX

THE one that could repeat the summer day
Were greater than itself, though he
Minutest of mankind might be.
And who could reproduce the sun,
At period of going down—
The lingering and the stain, I mean—
When Orient has been outgrown,
And Occident becomes unknown,
His name remain.

XXX

THE wind tapped like a tired man,
And like a host, "Come in,"
I boldly answered; entered then
My residence within

---

*Extremely hard stone; unbreakable or extremely hard substance.

A rapid, footless guest,
To offer whom a chair
Were as impossible as hand
A sofa to the air.

No bone had he to bind him,
His speech was like the push
Of numerous humming-birds at once
From a superior bush.

His countenance a billow,
His fingers, if he pass,
Let go a music, as of tunes
Blown tremulous in glass.

He visited, still flitting;
Then, like a timid man,
Again he tapped—'t was flurriedly—
And I became alone.

XXXI

NATURE rarer uses yellow
    Than another hue;
Saves she all of that for sunsets,—
    Prodigal of blue,

Spending scarlet like a woman,
    Yellow she affords
Only scantly and selectly,
    Like a lover's words.

XXXII

THE leaves, like women, interchange
    Sagacious confidence;
Somewhat of nods, and somewhat of
    Portentous inference,

The parties in both cases
    Enjoining secrecy, —
Inviolable compact
    To notoriety.

XXXIII

How happy is the little stone
That rambles in the road alone,
And doesn't care about careers,
And exigencies* never fears;
Whose coat of elemental brown
A passing universe put on;
And independent as the sun,
Associates or glows alone,
Fulfilling absolute decree
In casual simplicity.

XXXIV

IT sounded as if the streets were running,
And then the streets stood still.

---

*Urgent states of affairs.

Eclipse was all we could see at the window,
And awe was all we could feel.

By and by the boldest stole out of his covert,
To see if time was there.
Nature was in her beryl* apron,
Mixing fresher air.

XXXV

THE rat is the concisest tenant.
He pays no rent, —
Repudiates the obligation,
On schemes intent.

Balking our wit
To sound or circumvent,
Hate cannot harm
A foe so reticent.

Neither decree
Prohibits him,
Lawful as
Equilibrium.

XXXVI

FREQUENTLY the woods are pink,
Frequently are brown;

---

*Variably colored, transparent to translucent glassy mineral.

Frequently the hills undress
Behind my native town.

Oft a head is crested
I was wont to see,
And as oft a cranny
Where it used to be.

And the earth, they tell me,
On its axis turned, —
Wonderful rotation
By but twelve performed!

XXXVII

THE wind begun to rock the grass
With threatening tunes and low, —
He flung a menace at the earth,
A menace at the sky.

The leaves unhooked themselves from trees
And started all abroad;
The dust did scoop itself like hands
And throw away the road.

The wagons quickened on the streets,
The thunder hurried slow;
The lightning showed a yellow beak,
And then a livid claw.

The birds put up the bars to nests,
The cattle fled to barns;
There came one drop of giant rain,
And then, as if the hands

That held the dams had parted hold,
The waters wrecked the sky,
But overlooked my father's house,
Just quartering a tree.

XXXVIII

SOUTH winds jostle them,
Bumblebees come,
Hover, hesitate,
Drink, and are gone.

Butterflies pause
On their passage Cashmere;
I, softly plucking,
Present them here!

· XXXIX·

BRING me the sunset in a cup,
Reckon the morning's flagons* up,
　　And say how many dew;
Tell me how far the morning leaps,
Tell me what time the weaver sleeps
　　Who spun the breadths of blue!

Write me how many notes there be
In the new robin's ecstasy
　　Among astonished boughs;
How many trips the tortoise makes,

---

*Large vessels for holding wine or other drinks.

How many cups the bee partakes, —
 The debauchee of dews!

Also, who laid the rainbow's piers,
Also, who leads the docile spheres
 By withes of supple blue?
Whose fingers string the stalactite,
Who counts the wampum* of the night,
 To see that none is due?

Who built this little Alban house
And shut the windows down so close
 My spirit cannot see?
Who'll let me out some gala day,
With implements to fly away,
 Passing pomposity?

XL

SHE sweeps with many-colored brooms,
And leaves the shreds behind;
Oh, housewife in the evening west,
Come back, and dust the pond!

You dropped a purple ravelling† in,
You dropped an amber thread;
And now you've littered all the East
With duds of emerald!

And still she plies her spotted brooms,
And still the aprons fly,

---

*Beads of polished shells strung in strands and used by Native Americans as money, ceremonial pledges, or ornaments.
†Loose thread.

Till brooms fade softly into stars —
And then I come away.

XLI

LIKE mighty footlights burned the red
At bases of the trees, —
The far theatricals of day
Exhibiting to these.

'T was universe that did applaud
While, chiefest of the crowd,
Enabled by his royal dress,
Myself distinguished God.

XLII

WHERE ships of purple gently toss
On seas of daffodil,
Fantastic sailors mingle,
And then — the wharf is still.

XLIII

BLAZING in gold and quenching in purple,
Leaping like leopards to the sky,
Then at the feet of the old horizon
Laying her spotted face, to die;

Stooping as low as the kitchen window,
Touching the roof and tinting the barn,
Kissing her bonnet to the meadow, —
And the juggler of day is gone!

XLIV

FARTHER in summer than the birds,
Pathetic from the grass,
A minor nation celebrates
Its unobtrusive mass.

No ordinance* is seen,
So gradual the grace,
A pensive custom it becomes,
Enlarging loneliness.

Antiquest† felt at noon
When August, burning low,
Calls forth this spectral canticle,‡
Repose to typify.

Remit as yet no grace,
No furrow on the glow,
Yet a druidic§ difference
Enhances nature now.

---

*Authoritative decree.
†This word seems to be Dickinson's coinage.
‡Liturgical song.
§Druids were ancient Celtic priests associated with magic and wizardry.

XLV

As imperceptibly as grief
The summer lapsed away, —
Too imperceptible, at last,
To seem like perfidy.

A quietness distilled,
As twilight long begun,
Or Nature, spending with herself
Sequestered afternoon.

The dusk drew earlier in,
The morning foreign shone, —
A courteous, yet harrowing grace,
As guest who would be gone.

And thus, without a wing,
Or service of a keel,
Our summer made her light escape
Into the beautiful.

XLVI

It can't be summer, — that got through;
It's early yet for spring;
There's that long town of white to cross
Before the blackbirds sing.

It can't be dying, — it's too rouge, —
The dead shall go in white.

So sunset shuts my question down
With clasps of chrysolite.*

XLVII

THE gentian† weaves her fringes,
The maple's loom is red.
My departing blossoms
Obviate parade.

A brief, but patient illness,
An hour to prepare;
And one, below this morning,
Is where the angels are.

It was a short procession, —
The bobolink was there,
An aged bee addressed us,
And then we knelt in prayer.

We trust that she was willing, —
We ask that we may be.
Summer, sister, seraph,
Let us go with thee!

In the name of the bee
And of the butterfly
And of the breeze, amen!

---

*Also known as olivine, a greenish mineral.
†Blue-flowering herb.

XLVIII

GOD made a little gentian;
It tried to be a rose
And failed, and all the summer laughed.
But just before the snows
There came a purple creature
That ravished all the hill;
And summer hid her forehead,
And mockery was still.
The frosts were her condition;
The Tyrian* would not come
Until the North evoked it.
"Creator! shall I bloom?"

XLIX

BESIDES the autumn poets sing,
A few prosaic days
A little this side of the snow
And that side of the haze.

A few incisive mornings,
A few ascetic eves, —
Gone Mr. Bryant's golden-rod,†
And Mr. Thomson's‡ sheaves.

---

*Crimson or purple dye.
†American writer William Cullen Bryant (1794–1878) refers to this flower in his poem "The Death of the Flowers."
‡Scottish poet James Thomson (1700–1748), best known for his long poem *The Seasons.*

Still is the bustle in the brook,
Sealed are the spicy valves;
Mesmeric fingers softly touch
The eyes of many elves.

Perhaps a squirrel may remain,
My sentiments to share.
Grant me, O Lord, a sunny mind,
Thy windy will to bear!

L

IT sifts from leaden sieves,
It powders all the wood,
It fills with alabaster wool
The wrinkles of the road.

It makes an even face
Of mountain and of plain, —
Unbroken forehead from the east
Unto the east again.

It reaches to the fence,
It wraps it, rail by rail,
Till it is lost in fleeces;
It flings a crystal veil

On stump and stack and stem, —
The summer's empty room,
Acres of seams where harvests were,
Recordless, but for them.

It ruffles wrists of posts,
As ankles of a queen, —

Then stills its artisans like ghosts,
Denying they have been.

LI

No brigadier throughout the year
So civic as the Jay.
A neighbor and a warrior too,
With shrill felicity

Pursuing winds that censure us
A February day,
The brother of the universe
Was never blown away.

The snow and he are intimate;
I've often seen them play
When heaven looked upon us all
With such severity,

I felt apology were due
To an insulted sky,
Whose pompous frown was nutriment
To their temerity.

The pillow of this daring head
Is pungent evergreens;
His larder—terse and militant—
Unknown, refreshing things;

His character a tonic,
His future a dispute;
Unfair an immortality
That leaves this neighbor out.

LII

New feet within my garden go,
New fingers stir the sod;
A troubadour upon the elm
Betrays the solitude.

New children play upon the green,
New weary sleep below;
And still the pensive spring returns,
And still the punctual snow!

LIII

Pink, small, and punctual.
Aromatic, low,
Covert in April,
Candid in May,

Dear to the moss,
Known by the knoll,
Next to the robin
In every human soul.

Bold little beauty,
Bedecked with thee,
Nature forswears
Antiquity.

(With the first Arbutus.)*

---

*Creeping plant with fragrant white or pink flowers.

LIV

THE murmur of a bee
A witchcraft yieldeth me.
If any ask me why,
'T were easier to die
Than tell.

The red upon the hill
Taketh away my will;
If anybody sneer,
Take care, for God is here,
That's all.

The breaking of the day
Addeth to my degree;
If any ask me how,
Artist, who drew me so,
Must tell!

LV

PERHAPS you'd like to buy a flower?
But I could never sell.
If you would like to borrow
Until the daffodil

Unties her yellow bonnet
Beneath the village door,
Until the bees, from clover rows
Their hock* and sherry draw,

---

*Rhine wine.

Why, I will lend until just then,
But not an hour more!

LVI

THE pedigree of honey
Does not concern the bee;
A clover, any time, to him
Is aristocracy.

LVII

SOME keep the Sabbath going to church;
I keep it staying at home,
With a bobolink for a chorister,
And an orchard for a dome.

Some keep the Sabbath in surplice;*
I just wear my wings,
And instead of tolling the bell for church,
Our little sexton† sings.

God preaches,—a noted clergyman,—
And the sermon is never long;
So instead of getting to heaven at last,
I'm going all along!

---

*Loose white ecclesiastical vestment with large open sleeves.
†Church officer who tends church property and performs minor duties, such as ringing the bell for services.

LVIII

THE bee is not afraid of me,
I know the butterfly;
The pretty people in the woods
Receive me cordially.

The brooks laugh louder when I come,
The breezes madder play.
Wherefore, mine eyes, thy silver mists?
Wherefore, O summer's day?

LIX

SOME rainbow coming from the fair!
Some vision of the World Cashmere
I confidently see!
Or else a peacock's purple train,
Feather by feather, on the plain
Fritters itself away!

The dreamy butterflies bestir,
Lethargic pools resume the whir
Of last year's sundered tune.
From some old fortress on the sun
Baronial bees march, one by one,
In murmuring platoon!

The robins stand as thick to-day
As flakes of snow stood yesterday,
On fence and roof and twig.

The orchis* binds her feather on
For her old lover, Don† the Sun,
Revisiting the bog!

Without commander, countless, still,
The regiment of wood and hill
In bright detachment stand.
Behold! Whose multitudes are these?
The children of whose turbaned seas,
Or what Circassian‡ land?

LX

THE grass so little has to do, —
A sphere of simple green,
With only butterflies to brood,
And bees to entertain,

And stir all day to pretty tunes
The breezes fetch along,
And hold the sunshine in its lap
And bow to everything;

And thread the dews all night, like pearls,
And make itself so fine, —
A duchess were too common
For such a noticing.

And even when it dies, to pass
In odors so divine,

---

*Orchid.
†Title for a gentleman (Spanish).
‡Of a region of southwestern Russia on the coast of the Black Sea.

As lowly spices gone to sleep,
Or amulets* of pine.

And then to dwell in sovereign barns,
And dream the days away, —
The grass so little has to do,
I wish I were a hay!

LXI

A little road not made of man,
Enabled of the eye,
Accessible to thill† of bee,
Or cart of butterfly.

If town it have, beyond itself,
'T is that I cannot say;
I only sigh, — no vehicle
Bears me along that way.

LXII

A drop fell on the apple tree.
Another on the roof;
A half a dozen kissed the eaves,
And made the gables‡ laugh.

---

*Protective charms.
†Shaft of a vehicle.
‡Vertical triangular ends of a building extending from the cornice or eaves to the ridge of the roof.

A few went out to help the brook,
That went to help the sea.
Myself conjectured, Were they pearls,
What necklaces could be!

The dust replaced in hoisted roads,
The birds jocoser* sung;
The sunshine threw his hat away,
The orchards spangles hung.

The breezes brought dejected lutes,
And bathed them in the glee;
The East put out a single flag,
And signed the fête† away.

LXIII

A something in a summer's day,
As slow her flambeaux‡ burn away,
Which solemnizes me.

A something in a summer's noon,—
An azure depth, a wordless tune,
Transcending ecstasy.

And still within a summer's night
A something so transporting bright,
I clap my hands to see;

---

*More happily.
†Festival.
‡Flaming torches.

Then veil my too inspecting face,
Lest such a subtle, shimmering grace
Flutter too far for me.

The wizard-fingers never rest,
The purple brook within the breast
Still chafes its narrow bed;

Still rears the East her amber flag,
Guides still the sun along the crag
His caravan of red,

Like flowers that heard the tale of dews,
But never deemed the dripping prize
Awaited their low brows;

Or bees, that thought the summer's name
Some rumor of delirium
No summer could for them;

Or Arctic creature, dimly stirred
By tropic hint,—some travelled bird
Imported to the wood;

Or wind's bright signal to the ear,
Making that homely and severe,
Contented, known, before

The heaven unexpected came,
To lives that thought their worshipping
A too presumptuous psalm.

LXIV

THIS is the land the sunset washes,
These are the banks of the Yellow Sea;*
Where it rose, or whither it rushes,
These are the western mystery!

Night after night her purple traffic
Strews the landing with opal† bales;
Merchantmen poise upon horizons,
Dip, and vanish with fairy sails.

LXV

LIKE trains of cars on tracks of plush
I hear the level bee:
A jar across the flowers goes,
Their velvet masonry

Withstands until the sweet assault
Their chivalry consumes,
While he, victorious, tilts away
To vanquish other blooms.

His feet are shod with gauze,
His helmet is of gold;
His breast, a single onyx‡
With chrysoprase,§ inlaid.

---

*Inlet of the East China Sea.
†Meaning iridescent; an opal is an iridescent mineral.
‡Translucent quartz in parallel layers of different colors.
§Apple-green quartz.

His labor is a chant,
His idleness a tune;
Oh, for a bee's experience
Of clovers and of noon!

LXVI

THERE is a flower that bees prefer,
And butterflies desire;
To gain the purple democrat
The humming-birds aspire.

And whatsoever insect pass,
A honey bears away
Proportioned to his several dearth
And her capacity.

Her face is rounder than the moon,
And ruddier than the gown
Of orchis in the pasture,
Or rhododendron worn.

She doth not wait for June;
Before the world is green
Her sturdy little countenance
Against the wind is seen,

Contending with the grass,
Near kinsman to herself,
For privilege of sod and sun,
Sweet litigants for life.

And when the hills are full,
And newer fashions blow,

Doth not retract a single spice
For pang of jealousy.

Her public is the noon,
Her providence the sun,
Her progress by the bee proclaimed
In sovereign, swerveless tune.

The bravest of the host,
Surrendering the last,
Nor even of defeat aware
When cancelled by the frost.

LXVII

PRESENTIMENT is that long shadow on the lawn
Indicative that suns go down;
The notice to the startled grass
That darkness is about to pass.

LXVIII

As children bid the guest good-night,
And then reluctant turn,
My flowers raise their pretty lips,
Then put their nightgowns on.

As children caper when they wake,
Merry that it is morn,
My flowers from a hundred cribs
Will peep, and prance again.

LXIX

ANGELS in the early morning
May be seen the dews among,
Stooping, plucking, smiling, flying:
Do the buds to them belong?

Angels when the sun is hottest
May be seen the sands among,
Stooping, plucking, sighing, flying;
Parched the flowers they bear along.

LXX

So bashful when I spied her,
So pretty, so ashamed!
So hidden in her leaflets,
Lest anybody find;

So breathless till I passed her,
So helpless when I turned
And bore her, struggling, blushing,
Her simple haunts beyond!

For whom I robbed the dingle,*
For whom betrayed the dell,†
Many will doubtless ask me,
But I shall never tell!

---

*Small wooded valley.
†Secluded hollow or small valley.

LXXI

IT makes no difference abroad,
The seasons fit the same,
The mornings blossom into noons,
And split their pods of flame.

Wild-flowers kindle in the woods,
The brooks brag all the day;
No blackbird bates* his jargoning
For passing Calvary.

Auto-da-fé† and judgment
Are nothing to the bee;
His separation from his rose
To him seems misery.

LXXII

THE mountain sat upon the plain
In his eternal chair,
His observation omnifold,‡
His inquest everywhere.

The seasons prayed around his knees,
Like children round a sire:
Grandfather of the days is he,
Of dawn the ancestor.

---

*Restrains, lessens in intensity.
†Ceremony accompanying judgment by the Inquisition; the burning of a heretic.
‡Dickinson's coinage, meaning "reaching everywhere."

LXXIII

I'LL tell you how the sun rose,—
A ribbon at a time.
The steeples swam in amethyst,
The news like squirrels ran.

The hills untied their bonnets,
The bobolinks begun.
Then I said softly to myself,
"That must have been the sun!"

* * * * * *

But how he set, I know not.
There seemed a purple stile
Which little yellow boys and girls
Were climbing all the while

Till when they reached the other side,
A dominie* in gray
Put gently up the evening bars,
And led the flock away.

LXXIV

THE butterfly's assumption-gown,†
In chrysoprase apartments hung,
 This afternoon put on.

How condescending to descend,
And be of buttercups the friend
 In a New England town!

---

*Schoolmaster or clergyman.
†Assumption is the process of being taken up to heaven.

LXXV

OF all the sounds despatched abroad,
There's not a charge to me
Like that old measure in the boughs,
That phraseless melody

The wind does, working like a hand
Whose fingers comb the sky,
Then quiver down, with tufts of tune
Permitted gods and me.

When winds go round and round in bands,
And thrum* upon the door,
And birds take places overhead,
To bear them orchestra,

I crave him grace, of summer boughs,
If such an outcast be,
He never heard that fleshless chant
Rise solemn in the tree,

As if some caravan of sound
On deserts, in the sky,
Had broken rank,
Then knit, and passed
In seamless company.

LXXVI

APPARENTLY with no surprise
To any happy flower,

---

*Strum, or make a monotonous humming sound.

The frost beheads it at its play
In accidental power.

The blond assassin passes on,
The sun proceeds unmoved
To measure off another day
For an approving God.

LXXVII

'Twas later when the summer went
Than when the cricket came,
And yet we knew that gentle clock
Meant nought but going home.

'T was sooner when the cricket went
Than when the winter came,
Yet that pathetic pendulum
Keeps esoteric time.

LXXVIII

THESE are the days when birds come back,
A very few, a bird or two,
To take a backward look.

These are the days when skies put on
The old, old sophistries* of June, —
A blue and gold mistake.

---

*Subtly deceptive reasons or arguments.

Oh, fraud that cannot cheat the bee,
Almost thy plausibility
Induces my belief,

Till ranks of seeds their witness bear,
And softly through the altered air
Hurries a timid leaf!

Oh, sacrament of summer days,
Oh, last communion in the haze,
Permit a child to join,

Thy sacred emblems to partake,
Thy consecrated bread to break,
Taste thine immortal wine!

LXXIX

THE morns are meeker than they were,
The nuts are getting brown;
The berry's cheek is plumper,
The rose is out of town.

The maple wears a gayer scarf,
The field a scarlet gown.
Lest I should be old-fashioned,
I'll put a trinket on.

LXXX

THE sky is low, the clouds are mean,
A travelling flake of snow

Across a barn or through a rut
Debates if it will go.

A narrow wind complains all day
How some one treated him;
Nature, like us, is sometimes caught
Without her diadem.

LXXXI

I think the hemlock likes to stand
Upon a marge* of snow;
It suits his own austerity,
And satisfies an awe

That men must slake in wilderness,
Or in the desert cloy, —
An instinct for the hoar, the bald,
Lapland's necessity.

The hemlock's nature thrives on cold;
The gnash of northern winds
Is sweetest nutriment to him,
His best Norwegian wines.

To satin races he is nought;
But children on the Don†
Beneath his tabernacles‡ play,
And Dnieper wrestlers run.

---

*Margin (archaic).
†The Don and the Dnieper (mentioned two lines down) are rivers in Russia.
‡A tabernacle is a tent sanctuary; also a house of worship.

LXXXII

THERE'S a certain slant of light,
On winter afternoons,
That oppresses, like the weight
Of cathedral tunes.

Heavenly hurt it gives us;
We can find no scar,
But internal difference
Where the meanings are.

None may teach it anything,
'T is the seal,* despair, —
An imperial affliction
Sent us of the air.

When it comes, the landscape listens,
Shadows hold their breath;
When it goes, 't is like the distance
On the look of death.

LXXXIII

THE springtime's pallid landscape
    Will glow like bright bouquet,
Though drifted deep in parian†
    The village lies to-day.

---

*Here and elsewhere in Dickinson's work, "seal" likely has biblical resonance, as in the Seven Seals of the Apocalypse (see Revelation 5).
†Porcelain.

The lilacs, bending many a year,
　　With purple load will hang;
The bees will not forget the tune
　　Their old forefathers sang.

The rose will redden in the bog,
　　The aster on the hill
Her everlasting fashion set,
　　And covenant gentians frill,

Till summer folds her miracle
　　As women do their gown,
Or priests adjust the symbols
　　When sacrament is done.

LXXXIV

SHE slept beneath a tree
Remembered but by me.
I touched her cradle mute;
She recognized the foot,
Put on her carmine suit, —
　　And see!

(With a Tulip.)

LXXXV

A light exists in spring
　　Not present on the year
At any other period.
　　When March is scarcely here

A color stands abroad
    On solitary hills
That science cannot overtake,
    But human nature *feels*.

It waits upon the lawn;
    It shows the furthest tree
Upon the furthest slope we know;
    It almost speaks to me.

Then, as horizons step,
    Or noons report away,
Without the formula of sound,
    It passes, and we stay:

A quality of loss
    Affecting our content,
As trade had suddenly encroached
    Upon a sacrament.

LXXXVI

A lady red upon the hill
    Her annual secret keeps;
A lady white within the field
    In placid lily sleeps!

The tidy breezes with their brooms
    Sweep vale, and hill, and tree!
Prithee, my pretty housewives!
    Who may expected be?

The neighbors do not yet suspect!
    The woods exchange a smile —

Orchard, and buttercup, and bird—
   In such a little while!

And yet how still the landscape stands,
   How nonchalant the wood,
As if the resurrection
   Were nothing very odd!

LXXXVII

DEAR March, come in!
How glad I am!
I looked for you before.
Put down your hat—
You must have walked—
How out of breath you are!
Dear March, how are you?
And the rest?
Did you leave Nature well?
Oh, March, come right upstairs with me,
I have so much to tell!

I got your letter, and the bird's;
The maples never knew
That you were coming,—I declare,
How red their faces grew!
But, March, forgive me—
And all those hills
You left for me to hue;
There was no purple suitable,
You took it all with you.

Who knocks? That April!
Lock the door!
I will not be pursued!

He stayed away a year, to call
When I am occupied.
But trifles look so trivial
As soon as you have come,
That blame is just as dear as praise
And praise as mere as blame.

LXXXVIII

WE like March, his shoes are purple,
    He is new and high;
Makes he mud for dog and peddler,
    Makes he forest dry;
Knows the adder's tongue his coming,
    And begets her spot.
Stands the sun so close and mighty
    That our minds are hot.
News is he of all the others;
    Bold it were to die
With the blue-birds buccaneering
    On his British sky.

LXXXIX

NOT knowing when the dawn will come
    I open every door;
Or has it feathers like a bird,
    Or billows like a shore?

XC

A murmur in the trees to note,
    Not loud enough for wind;
A star not far enough to seek,
    Nor near enough to find;

A long, long yellow on the lawn,
    A hubbub as of feet;
Not audible, as ours to us,
    But dapperer, more sweet;

A hurrying home of little men
    To houses unperceived, —
All this, and more, if I should tell,
    Would never be believed.

Of robins in the trundle bed
    How many I espy
Whose nightgowns could not hide the wings,
    Although I heard them try!

But then I promised ne'er to tell;
    How could I break my word?
So go your way and I'll go mine, —
    No fear you'll miss the road.

XCI

MORNING is the place for dew,
    Corn is made at noon,
After dinner light for flowers,
    Dukes for setting sun!

XCII

To my quick ear the leaves conferred;
    The bushes they were bells;
I could not find a privacy
    From Nature's sentinels.

In cave if I presumed to hide,
    The walls began to tell;
Creation seemed a mighty crack
    To make me visible.

XCIII

A sepal,* petal, and a thorn
Upon a common summer's morn,
A flash of dew, a bee or two,
A breeze
A caper in the trees, —
    And I'm a rose!

XCIV

HIGH from the earth I heard a bird;
    He trod upon the trees
As he esteemed them trifles,
    And then he spied a breeze,
And situated softly
    Upon a pile of wind

---

*One of the leaves composing the calyx of a flower.

Which in a perturbation
    Nature had left behind.
A joyous-going fellow
    I gathered from his talk,
Which both of benediction
    And badinage partook,
Without apparent burden,
    I learned, in leafy wood
He was the faithful father
    Of a dependent brood;
And this untoward transport
    His remedy for care, —
A contrast to our respites.
    How different we are!

XCV

THE spider as an artist
    Has never been employed
Though his surpassing merit
    Is freely certified

By every broom and Bridget*
    Throughout a Christian land.
Neglected son of genius,
    I take thee by the hand.

XCVI

WHAT mystery pervades a well!
    The water lives so far,

---

*A patron saint of Ireland; founder of several convents.

Like neighbor from another world
      Residing in a jar.

The grass does not appear afraid;
      I often wonder he
Can stand so close and look so bold
      At what is dread to me.

Related somehow they may be, —
      The sedge* stands next the sea,
Where he is floorless, yet of fear
      No evidence gives he.

But nature is a stranger yet;
      The ones that cite her most
Have never passed her haunted house,
      Nor simplified her ghost.

To pity those that know her not
      Is helped by the regret
That those who know her, know her less
      The nearer her they get.

XCVII

To make a prairie it takes a clover
and one bee, —
One clover, and a bee,
And revery.
The revery alone will do
If bees are few.

---

*Tufted marsh plant.

XCVIII

It's like the light,—
    A fashionless delight,
It's like the bee,—
    A dateless melody.

It's like the woods,
    Private like breeze,
Phraseless, yet it stirs
    The proudest trees.

It's like the morning,—
    Best when it's done,—
The everlasting clocks
    Chime noon.

XCIX

A dew sufficed itself
    And satisfied a leaf,
And felt, "how vast a destiny!
    How trivial is life!"

The sun went out to work,
    The day went out to play,
But not again that dew was seen
    By physiognomy.

Whether by day abducted,
    Or emptied by the sun
Into the sea, in passing,
    Eternally unknown.

C

His bill an auger* is,
　　His head, a cap and frill.
He laboreth at every tree, —
　　A worm his utmost goal.

CI

Sweet is the swamp with its secrets,
　　Until we meet a snake;
'T is then we sigh for houses,
　　And our departure take

At that enthralling gallop
　　That only childhood knows.
A snake is summer's treason,
　　And guile is where it goes.

CII

Could I but ride indefinite,
　　As doth the meadow-bee,
And visit only where I liked,
　　And no man visit me,

And flirt all day with buttercups,
　　And marry whom I may,

---

*Tool for boring holes.

And dwell a little everywhere,
    Or better, run away

With no police to follow,
    Or chase me if I do,
Till I should jump peninsulas
    To get away from you, —

I said, but just to be a bee
    Upon a raft of air,
And row in nowhere all day long,
    And anchor off the bar, —
What liberty! So captives deem
    Who tight in dungeons are

CIII

THE moon was but a chin of gold
    A night or two ago,
And now she turns her perfect face
    Upon the world below.

Her forehead is of amplest blond;
    Her cheek like beryl stone;
Her eye unto the summer dew
    The likest I have known.

Her lips of amber never part;
    But what must be the smile
Upon her friend she could bestow
    Were such her silver will!

And what a privilege to be
    But the remotest star!

For certainly her way might pass
    Beside your twinkling door.

Her bonnet is the firmament,
    The universe her shoe,
The stars the trinkets at her belt,
    Her dimities of blue.

CIV

THE bat is dun with wrinkled wings
    Like fallow article,
And not a song pervades his lips,
    Or none perceptible.

His small umbrella, quaintly halved,
    Describing in the air
An arc alike inscrutable, —
    Elate* philosopher!

Deputed from what firmament
    Of what astute abode,
Empowered with what malevolence
    Auspiciously withheld.

To his adroit Creator
    Ascribe no less the praise;
Beneficent, believe me,
    His eccentricities.

---

*Elated.

CV

YOU'VE seen balloons set, haven't you?
　　So stately they ascend
It is as swans discarded you
　　For duties diamond.

Their liquid feet go softly out
　　Upon a sea of blond;
They spurn the air as 't were to mean
　　For creatures so renowned.

Their ribbons just beyond the eye,
　　They struggle some for breath,
And yet the crowd applauds below;
　　They would not encore death.

The gilded creature strains and spins,
　　Trips frantic in a tree,
Tears open her imperial veins
　　And tumbles in the sea.

The crowd retire with an oath
　　The dust in streets goes down,
And clerks in counting-rooms observe,
　　" 'T was only a balloon."

CVI

THE cricket sang,
And set the sun,
And workmen finished, one by one,
　　Their seam the day upon.

The low grass loaded with the dew,
The twilight stood as strangers do
With hat in hand, polite and new,
　　To stay as if, or go.

A vastness, as a neighbor, came,—
A wisdom without face or name,
A peace, as hemispheres at home,—
　　And so the night became.

CVII

DRAB habitation of whom?
Tabernacle or tomb,
Or dome of worm,
Or porch of gnome,
Or some elf's catacomb?

(Sent with a cocoon to her little nephew.)

CVIII

A sloop* of amber slips away
　　Upon an ether sea,
And wrecks in peace a purple tar,
　　The son of ecstasy.

---

*A fore- and aft-rigged boat.

CIX

OF bronze and blaze
The north, to-night!
    So adequate its forms,
So preconcerted with itself,
    So distant to alarms, —
An unconcern so sovereign
    To universe, or me,
It paints my simple spirit
    With tints of majesty,
Till I take vaster attitudes,
    And strut upon my stem,
Disdaining men and oxygen,
    For arrogance of them.

My splendors are menagerie;
    But their competeless show
Will entertain the centuries
    When I am, long ago,
An island in dishonored grass,
    Whom none but daisies know.

CX

How the old mountains drip with sunset,
    And the brake of dun!
How the hemlocks are tipped in tinsel
    By the wizard sun!

How the old steeples hand the scarlet,
    Till the ball is full, —
Have I the lip of the flamingo
    That I dare to tell?

Then, how the fire ebbs like billows,
    Touching all the grass
With a departing, sapphire feature,
    As if a duchess pass!

How a small dusk crawls on the village
    Till the houses blot;
And the odd flambeaux no men carry
    Glimmer on the spot!

Now it is night in nest and kennel,
    And where was the wood,
Just a dome of abyss is nodding
    Into solitude! —

These are the visions baffled Guido;
    Titian never told;
Domenichino* dropped the pencil,
    Powerless to unfold.

CXI

THE murmuring of bees has ceased;
    But murmuring of some
Posterior, prophetic,
    Has simultaneous come, —

The lower metres of the year,
    When nature's laugh is done, —
The Revelations of the book
    Whose Genesis in June.

---

*Guido Reni (1575–1642), Italian painter known for his religious and mytholog-
ical subjects. Tiziano Vicellio (1485?–1576), Italian painter renowned for his use
of color. Italian painter (1581–1641), a leader of the Baroque eclectic school; also
known as Domenico Zampieri.

PART THREE

LOVE

IT's all I have to bring to-day,
    This, and my heart beside,
This, and my heart, and all the fields,
    And all the meadows wide.
Be sure you count, should I forget, —
    Some one the sun could tell, —
This, and my heart, and all the bees
    Which in the clover dwell.

I

MINE by the right of the white election!
Mine by the royal seal!
Mine by the sign in the scarlet prison
Bars cannot conceal!

Mine, here in vision and in veto!
Mine, by the grave's repeal
Titled, confirmed, — delirious charter!
Mine, while the ages steal!

II

YOU left me, sweet, two legacies, —
A legacy of love
A Heavenly Father would content,
Had He the offer of;

You left me boundaries of pain
Capacious as the sea,
Between eternity and time,
Your consciousness and me.

III

ALTER? When the hills do.
Falter? When the sun

Question if his glory
Be the perfect one.

Surfeit? When the daffodil
Doth of the dew:
Even as herself, O friend!
I will of you!

IV

Elysium* is as far as to
The very nearest room,
If in that room a friend await
Felicity or doom.

What fortitude the soul contains,
That it can so endure
The accent of a coming foot,
The opening of a door!

V

Doubt me, my dim companion!
Why, God would be content
With but a fraction of the love
Poured thee without a stint.†
The whole of me, forever,
What more the woman can, —

---

*In Greek mythology, the home of the blessed after death.
†Cease.

Say quick, that I may dower* thee
With last delight I own!

It cannot be my spirit,
For that was thine before;
I ceded all of dust I knew, —
What opulence the more
Had I, a humble maiden,
Whose farthest of degree
Was that she might
Some distant heaven,
Dwell timidly with thee!

VI

IF you were coming in the fall,
I'd brush the summer by
With half a smile and half a spurn,
As housewives do a fly.

If I could see you in a year,
I'd wind the months in balls,
And put them each in separate drawers,
Until their time befalls.

If only centuries delayed,
I'd count them on my hand,
Subtracting till my fingers dropped
Into Van Diemen's land.†

If certain, when this life was out,
That yours and mine should be,

---

*Endow.
†Tasmania; founded as a penal colony in the early 1800s.

I'd toss it yonder like a rind,
And taste eternity.

But now, all ignorant of the length
Of time's uncertain wing,
It goads me, like the goblin bee,
That will not state its sting.

VII

I hide myself within my flower,
That wearing on your breast,
You, unsuspecting, wear me too—
And angels know the rest.

I hide myself within my flower,
That, fading from your vase,
You, unsuspecting, feel for me
Almost a loneliness.

VIII

THAT I did always love,
I bring thee proof:
That till I loved
I did not love enough.

That I shall love alway,
I offer thee
That love is life,
And life hath immortality.

This, dost thou doubt, sweet?
Then have I
Nothing to show
But Calvary.

IX

HAVE you got a brook in your little heart,
Where bashful flowers blow,
And blushing birds go down to drink,
And shadows tremble so?

And nobody knows, so still it flows,
That any brook is there;
And yet your little draught of life
Is daily drunken there.

Then look out for the little brook in March,
When the rivers overflow,
And the snows come hurrying from the hills,
And the bridges often go.

And later, in August it may be,
When the meadows parching lie,
Beware, lest this little brook of life
Some burning noon go dry!

X

As if some little Arctic flower,
Upon the polar hem,
Went wandering down the latitudes,

Until it puzzled came
To continents of summer,
To firmaments of sun,
To strange, bright crowds of flowers,
And birds of foreign tongue!
I say, as if this little flower
To Eden wandered in —
What then? Why, nothing, only
Your inference therefrom!

XI

My river runs to thee:
Blue sea, wilt welcome me?

My river waits reply.
Oh sea, look graciously!

I'll fetch thee brooks
From spotted nooks, —

Say, sea,
Take me!

XII

I cannot live with you,
It would be life,
And life is over there
Behind the shelf

The sexton keeps the key to,
Putting up
Our life, his porcelain,
Like a cup

Discarded of the housewife,
Quaint or broken;
A newer Sèvres* pleases,
Old ones crack.

I could not die with you,
For one must wait
To shut the other's gaze down, —
You could not.

And I, could I stand by
And see you freeze,
Without my right of frost,
Death's privilege?

Nor could I rise with you,
Because your face
Would put out Jesus',
That new grace

Glow plain and foreign
On my homesick eye,
Except that you, than he
Shone closer by.

They'd judge us — how?
For you served Heaven, you know,
Or sought to;
I could not,

---

*Fine French porcelain, often elaborately decorated.

Because you saturated sight,
And I had no more eyes
For sordid excellence
As Paradise.

And were you lost, I would be,
Though my name
Rang loudest
On the heavenly fame.

And were you saved,
And I condemned to be
Where you were not,
That self were hell to me.

So we must keep apart,
You there, I here,
With just the door ajar
That oceans are,
And prayer,
And that pale sustenance,
Despair!

XIII

THERE came a day at summer's full
Entirely for me;
I thought that such were for the saints,
Where revelations be.

The sun, as common, went abroad,
The flowers, accustomed, blew,
As if no sail the solstice passed
That maketh all things new.

The time was scarce profaned by speech;
The symbol of a word
Was needless, as at sacrament
The wardrobe of our Lord.

Each was to each the sealed church,
Permitted to commune this time,
Lest we too awkward show
At supper of the Lamb.*

The hours slid fast, as hours will,
Clutched tight by greedy hands;
So faces on two decks look back,
Bound to opposing lands.

And so, when all the time had failed,
Without external sound,
Each bound the other's crucifix,
We gave no other bond.

Sufficient troth that we shall rise —
Deposed, at length, the grave —
To that new marriage, justified
Through Calvaries of Love!

XIV

I'M ceded, I've stopped being theirs;
The name they dropped upon my face
With water, in the country church,
Is finished using now,

---

*A reference to the Bible, Revelation 19:9, describing a metaphorical marriage between the church and Jesus (the Lamb): "Blessed are they which are called unto the marriage supper of the Lamb" (KJV).

And they can put it with my dolls,
My childhood, and the string of spools
I've finished threading too.

Baptized before without the choice,
But this time consciously, of grace
Unto supremest name,
Called to my full, the crescent dropped,
Existence's whole arc filled up
With one small diadem.

My second rank, too small the first,
Crowned, crowing on my father's breast,
A half unconscious queen,
But this time, adequate, erect,
With will to choose or to reject,
And I choose — just a throne.

XV

'T was a long parting, but the time
For interview had come;
Before the judgment-seat of God,
The last and second time

These fleshless lovers met,
A heaven in a gaze,
A heaven of heavens, the privilege
Of one another's eyes.

No lifetime set on them,
Apparelled as the new
Unborn, except they had beheld,
Born everlasting now.

Was bridal* e'er like this?
A paradise, the host,
And cherubim and seraphim
The most familiar guest.

XVI

I'M wife; I've finished that,
That other state;
I'm Czar, I'm woman now:
It's safer so.

How odd the girl's life looks
Behind this soft eclipse!
I think that earth seems so
To those in heaven now.

This being comfort, then
That other kind was pain;
But why compare?
I'm wife! stop there!

XVII

SHE rose to his requirement, dropped
The playthings of her life
To take the honorable work
Of woman and of wife.

---

*Marriage ceremony.

If aught she missed in her new day
Of amplitude, or awe,
Or first prospective, or the gold
In using wore away,

It lay unmentioned, as the sea
Develops pearl and weed,
But only to himself is known
The fathoms they abide.

XVIII

COME slowly, Eden!
Lips unused to thee,
Bashful, sip thy jasmines,
As the fainting bee,

Reaching late his flower,
Round her chamber hums,
Counts his nectars—enters,
And is lost in balms!*

XIX

OF all the souls that stand create
I have elected one.
When sense from spirit files away,
And subterfuge is done;

---

*Pleasing fragrances.

When that which is and that which was
Apart, intrinsic, stand,
And this brief tragedy of flesh
Is shifted like a sand;

When figures show their royal front
And mists are carved away, —
Behold the atom I preferred
To all the lists* of clay!

XX

I have no life but this,
To lead it here;
Nor any death, but lest
Dispelled from there;

Nor tie to earths to come,
Nor action new,
Except through this extent,
The realm of you.

XXI

YOUR riches taught me poverty.
Myself a millionnaire
In little wealths, — as girls could boast, —
Till broad as Buenos Ayre,†

---

*Narrow strips.
†Buenos Aires, the capital of Argentina.

You drifted your dominions
A different Peru;
And I esteemed all poverty,
For life's estate with you.

Of mines I little know, myself,
But just the names of gems, —
The colors of the commonest;
And scarce of diadems

So much that, did I meet the queen,
Her glory I should know:
But this must be a different wealth,
To miss it beggars so.

I'm sure 't is India all day
To those who look on you
Without a stint, without a blame, —
Might I but be the Jew!

I'm sure it is Golconda,*
Beyond my power to deem, —
To have a smile for mine each day,
How better than a gem!

At least, it solaces to know
That there exists a gold,
Although I prove it just in time
Its distance to behold!

It's far, far treasure to surmise,
And estimate the pearl
That slipped my simple fingers through
While just a girl at school!

*Ruined city in south-central India, where diamonds from nearby mines were cut and sold during the fifteenth century.

XXII

I gave myself to him,
And took himself for pay.
The solemn contract of a life
Was ratified this way.

The wealth might disappoint,
Myself a poorer prove
Than this great purchaser suspect,
The daily own* of Love

Depreciate the vision;
But, till the merchant buy,
Still fable, in the isles of spice,
The subtle cargoes lie.

At least, 't is mutual risk, —
Some found it mutual gain;
Sweet debt of Life, — each night to owe,
Insolvent, every noon.

XXIII

"GOING to him! Happy letter! Tell him —
Tell him the page I didn't write;
Tell him I only said the syntax,
And left the verb and the pronoun out.
Tell him just how the fingers hurried,
Then how they waded, slow, slow, slow;

---

*Owning.

And then you wished you had eyes in your pages,
So you could see what moved them so.

"Tell him it wasn't a practised writer,
You guessed, from the way the sentence toiled;
You could hear the bodice tug, behind you,
As if it held but the might of a child;
You almost pitied it, you, it worked so.
Tell him— No, you may quibble there,
For it would split his heart to know it,
And then you and I were silenter.

"Tell him night finished before we finished,
And the old clock kept neighing 'day!'
And you got sleepy and begged to be ended—
What could it hinder so, to say?
Tell him just how she sealed you, cautious,
But if he ask where you are hid
Until to-morrow,—happy letter!
Gesture, coquette,* and shake your head!"

XXIV

THE way I read a letter's this:
'T is first I lock the door,
And push it with my fingers next,
For transport it be sure.

And then I go the furthest off
To counteract a knock;
Then draw my little letter forth
And softly pick its lock.

---

*Flirt.

Then, glancing narrow at the wall,
And narrow at the floor,
For firm conviction of a mouse
Not exorcised before,

Peruse how infinite I am
To—no one that you know!
And sigh for lack of heaven,—but not
The heaven the creeds bestow.

XXV

WILD nights! Wild nights!
Were I with thee,
Wild nights should be
Our luxury!

Futile the winds
To a heart in port,—
Done with the compass,
Done with the chart.

Rowing in Eden!
Ah! the sea!
Might I but moor
To-night in thee!

XXVI

THE night was wide, and furnished scant
With but a single star,
That often as a cloud it met
Blew out itself for fear.

The wind pursued the little bush,
And drove away the leaves
November left; then clambered up
And fretted in the eaves.

No squirrel went abroad;
A dog's belated feet
Like intermittent plush were heard
Adown the empty street.

To feel if blinds be fast,
And closer to the fire
Her little rocking-chair to draw,
And shiver for the poor,

The housewife's gentle task.
"How pleasanter," said she
Unto the sofa opposite,
"The sleet than May—no thee!"

XXVII

DID the harebell* loose her girdle
To the lover bee,
Would the bee the harebell hallow
Much as formerly?

Did the paradise, persuaded,
Yield her moat of pearl,
Would the Eden be an Eden,
Or the earl an earl?

---

*Plant with bell-shaped blue or white flowers.

XXVIII

A charm invests a face
Imperfectly beheld, —
The lady dare not lift her veil
For fear it be dispelled.

But peers beyond her mesh,
And wishes, and denies, —
Lest interview annul a want
That image satisfies.

XXIX

THE rose did caper on her cheek,
Her bodice rose and fell,
Her pretty speech, like drunken men,
Did stagger pitiful.

Her fingers fumbled at her work, —
Her needle would not go;
What ailed so smart a little maid
It puzzled me to know,

Till opposite I spied a cheek
That bore another rose;
Just opposite, another speech
That like the drunkard goes;

A vest that, like the bodice, danced
To the immortal tune, —
Till those two troubled little clocks
Ticked softly into one.

XXX

In lands I never saw, they say,
Immortal Alps look down,
Whose bonnets touch the firmament,
Whose sandals touch the town, —

Meek at whose everlasting feet
A myriad daisies play.
Which, sir, are you, and which am I,
Upon an August day?

XXXI

The moon is distant from the sea,
And yet with amber hands
She leads him, docile as a boy,
Along appointed sands.

He never misses a degree;
Obedient to her eye,
He comes just so far toward the town,
Just so far goes away.

Oh, Signor, thine the amber hand,
And mine the distant sea, —
Obedient to the least command
Thine eyes impose on me.

XXXII

He put the belt around my life, —
I heard the buckle snap,

And turned away, imperial,
My lifetime folding up
Deliberate, as a duke would do
A kingdom's title-deed, —
Henceforth a dedicated sort,
A member of the cloud.

Yet not too far to come at call,
And do the little toils
That make the circuit of the rest,
And deal occasional smiles
To lives that stoop to notice mine
And kindly ask it in, —
Whose invitation, knew you not
For whom I must decline?

XXXIII

I held a jewel in my fingers
And went to sleep.
The day was warm, and winds were prosy;
I said: " 'T will keep."

I woke and chid my honest fingers, —
The gem was gone;
And now an amethyst remembrance
Is all I own.

XXXIV

WHAT if I say I shall not wait?
What if I burst the fleshly gate

And pass, escaped, to thee?
What if I file this mortal off,
See where it hurt me,—that's enough,—
And wade in liberty?

They cannot take us any more,—
Dungeons may call, and guns implore;
Unmeaning now, to me,
As laughter was an hour ago,
Or laces, or a travelling show,
Or who died yesterday!

XXXV

PROUD of my broken heart since thou didst
    break it,
    Proud of the pain I did not feel till thee,
Proud of my night since thou with moons dost
    slake it,
    Not to partake thy passion, my humility.

XXXVI

My worthiness is all my doubt,
    His merit all my fear,
Contrasting which, my qualities
    Do lowlier appear;

Lest I should insufficient prove
    For his beloved need,
The chiefest apprehension
    Within my loving creed.

So I, the undivine abode
    Of his elect content,
Conform my soul as 't were a church
    Unto her sacrament.

XXXVII

LOVE is anterior to life,
    Posterior to death,
Initial of creation, and
    The exponent of breath.

XXXVIII

ONE blessing had I, than the rest
    So larger to my eyes
That I stopped gauging, satisfied,
    For this enchanted size.

It was the limit of my dream,
    The focus of my prayer, —
A perfect, paralyzing bliss
    Contented as despair.

I knew no more of want or cold,
    Phantasms both become,
For this new value in the soul,
    Supremest earthly sum.

The heaven below the heaven above
    Obscured with ruddier hue.

Life's latitude leant over-full;
    The judgment perished, too.

Why joys so scantily disburse,
    Why Paradise defer,
Why floods are served to us in bowls, —
    I speculate no more.

XXXIX

WHEN roses cease to bloom, dear,
    And violets are done,
When bumble-bees in solemn flight
    Have passed beyond the sun,

The hand that paused to gather
    Upon this summer's day
Will idle lie, in Auburn, — *
    Then take my flower, pray!

XL

SUMMER for thee grant I may be
    When summer days are flown!
Thy music still when whippoorwill
    And oriole are done!

For thee to bloom, I'll skip the tomb
    And sow my blossoms o'er!

---

*Reddish brown.

Pray gather me, Anemone,
    Thy flower forevermore!

XLI

Split the lark and you'll find the music,
    Bulb after bulb, in silver rolled,
Scantily dealt to the summer morning,
    Saved for your ear when lutes be old.

Loose the flood, you shall find it patent,
    Gush after gush, reserved for you;
Scarlet experiment! sceptic Thomas,*
    Now, do you doubt that your bird was true?

XLII

To lose thee, sweeter than to gain
    All other hearts I knew.
'T is true the drought is destitute,
    But then I had the dew!

The Caspian† has its realms of sand,
    Its other realm of sea;
Without the sterile perquisite‡
    No Caspian could be.

---

*The Apostle Thomas was at first skeptical that Jesus had risen (see the Bible, John 20:24–28).
†Caspian Sea, a saline lake between southeastern Europe and western Asia.
‡Extra payment or profit.

XLIII

Poor little heart!
Did they forget thee?
Then dinna* care! Then dinna care!

Proud little heart!
Did they forsake thee?
Be debonair! Be debonair!

Frail little heart!
I would not break thee:
Could'st credit me? Could'st credit me?

Gay little heart!
Like morning glory
Thou'll wilted be; thou'll wilted be!

XLIV

There is a word
Which bears a sword
  Can pierce an armed man.
It hurls its barbed syllables, —
  At once is mute again.
But where it fell
The saved will tell
  On patriotic day,
Some epauletted† brother
  Gave his breath away.
Wherever runs the breathless sun,

---

*Do not (Scottish dialect).
†Outfitted with shoulder ornaments, especially on military uniforms.

Wherever roams the day,
There is its noiseless onset,
    There is its victory!
Behold the keenest marksman!
    The most accomplished shot!
Time's sublimest target
    Is a soul "forgot"!

XLV

I'VE got an arrow here;
    Loving the hand that sent it,
I the dart revere.

Fell, they will say, in "skirmish"!
    Vanquished, my soul will know,
By but a simple arrow
    Sped by an archer's bow.

XLVI

HE fumbles at your spirit
    As players at the keys
Before they drop full music on;
    He stuns you by degrees,

Prepares your brittle substance
    For the ethereal blow,
By fainter hammers, further heard,
    Then nearer, then so slow

Your breath has time to straighten,
    Your brain to bubble cool,—

Deals one imperial thunderbolt
   That scalps your naked soul.

XLVII

HEART, we will forget him!
   You and I, to-night!
You may forget the warmth he gave,
   I will forget the light.

When you have done, pray tell me,
   That I my thoughts may dim;
Haste! lest while you're lagging,
   I may remember him!

XLVIII

FATHER, I bring thee not myself,—
   That were the little load;
I bring thee the imperial heart
   I had not strength to hold.

The heart I cherished in my own
   Till mine too heavy grew,
Yet strangest, heavier since it went,
   Is it too large for you?

XLIX

WE outgrow love like other things
   And put it in the drawer,

Till it an antique fashion shows
    Like costumes grandsires* wore.

L

Not with a club the heart is broken,
    Nor with a stone;
A whip, so small you could not see it,
    I've known

To lash the magic creature
    Till it fell,
Yet that whip's name too noble
    Then to tell.

Magnanimous of bird
    By boy descried,
To sing unto the stone
    Of which it died.

LI

My friend must be a bird,
    Because it flies!
Mortal my friend must be,
    Because it dies!
Barbs has it, like a bee.
Ah, curious friend,
    Thou puzzlest me!

---

*Male ancestors, forefathers.

LII

HE touched me, so I live to know
    That such a day, permitted so,
    I groped upon his breast.
It was a boundless place to me,
And silenced, as the awful sea
    Puts minor streams to rest.

And now, I'm different from before,
As if I breathed superior air,
    Or brushed a royal gown;
My feet, too, that had wandered so,
My gypsy face transfigured now
    To tenderer renown.

LIII

LET me not mar that perfect dream
    By an auroral* stain,
But so adjust my daily night
    That it will come again.

LIV

I live with him, I see his face;
    I go no more away

---

*Of the dawn.

For visitor, or sundown;
    Death's single privacy,

The only one forestalling mine,
    And that by right that he
Presents a claim invisible,
    No wedlock granted me.

I live with him, I hear his voice,
    I stand alive to-day
To witness to the certainty
    Of immortality

Taught me by Time, — the lower way,
    Conviction every day, —
That life like this is endless,
    Be judgment what it may.

LV

I envy seas whereon he rides,
    I envy spokes of wheels
Of chariots that him convey,
    I envy speechless hills

That gaze upon his journey;
    How easy all can see
What is forbidden utterly
    As heaven, unto me!

I envy nests of sparrows
    That dot his distant eaves,
The wealthy fly upon his pane,
    The happy, happy leaves

That just abroad his window
    Have summer's leave to be,

The earrings of Pizarro*
    Could not obtain for me.

I envy light that wakes him,
    And bells that boldly ring
To tell him it is noon abroad, —
    Myself his noon could bring,

Yet interdict my blossom
    And abrogate my bee,
Lest noon in everlasting night
    Drop Gabriel† and me.

LVI

A solemn thing it was, I said,
    A woman white‡ to be,
And wear, if God should count me fit,
    Her hallowed mystery,

A timid thing to drop a life
    Into the purple well,
Too plummetless that it come back
    Eternity until.

LVII

Title divine is mine
The Wife without

---

*Francisco Pizarro (c.1475–1541), Spanish explorer and conqueror of Peru.
†Archangel acting as the messenger of God (see the Bible, Luke 1:19).
‡A rare autobiographical note; Dickinson wore only white from her twenties on.

The Sign.
Acute degree
Conferred on me —
Empress of Calvary.
Royal all but the
Crown —
Betrothed, without the swoon
God gives us women
When two hold
Garnet to garnet,
Gold to gold —
Born — Bridalled —
Shrouded —
In a day
Tri-Victory —
        "My Husband"
Women say
Stroking the melody,
Is this the way?

PART FOUR

TIME AND ETERNITY

I

ONE dignity delays for all,
One mitred* afternoon.
None can avoid this purple,
None evade this crown.

Coach it insures, and footmen,
Chamber and state and throng;
Bells, also, in the village,
As we ride grand along.

What dignified attendants,
What service when we pause!
How loyally at parting
Their hundred hats they raise!

How pomp surpassing ermine,†
When simple you and I
Present our meek escutcheon,‡
And claim the rank to die!

II

DELAYED till she had ceased to know,
Delayed till in its vest of snow

---

*A miter is the liturgical headdress of a Christian bishop.
†Valuable white fur of a weasel.
‡Shield or shield-shaped emblem bearing a coat of arms.

Her loving bosom lay.
An hour behind the fleeting breath,
Later by just an hour than death, —
    Oh, lagging yesterday!

Could she have guessed that it would be;
Could but a crier of the glee
    Have climbed the distant hill;
Had not the bliss so slow a pace, —
Who knows but this surrendered face
    Were undefeated still?

Oh, if there may departing be
Any forgot by victory
    In her imperial round,
Show them this meek apparelled thing,
That could not stop to be a king,
    Doubtful if it be crowned!

III

DEPARTED to the judgment,
A mighty afternoon;
Great clouds like ushers leaning,
Creation looking on.

The flesh surrendered, cancelled,
The bodiless begun;
Two worlds, like audiences, disperse
And leave the soul alone.

IV

SAFE in their alabaster chambers,
Untouched by morning and untouched by noon,

Sleep the meek members of the resurrection,
Rafter of satin, and roof of stone.

Light laughs the breeze in her castle of sunshine;
Babbles the bee in a stolid ear;
Pipe the sweet birds in ignorant cadence, —
Ah, what sagacity perished here!

Grand go the years in the crescent above them;
Worlds scoop their arcs, and firmaments row,
Diadems drop and Doges* surrender,
Soundless as dots on a disk of snow.

V

On this long storm the rainbow rose,
On this late morn the sun;
The clouds, like listless elephants,
Horizons straggled down.

The birds rose smiling in their nests,
The gales indeed were done;
Alas! how heedless were the eyes
On whom the summer shone!

The quiet nonchalance of death
No daybreak can bestir;
The slow archangel's syllables
Must awaken her.

---

*Elected chief magistrates of the former republics of Venice and Genoa.

VI

My cocoon tightens, colors tease,
I'm feeling for the air;
A dim capacity for wings
Degrades the dress I wear.

A power of butterfly must be
The aptitude to fly,
Meadows of majesty concedes
And easy sweeps of sky.

So I must baffle at the hint
And cipher* at the sign,
And make much blunder, if at last
I take the clew† divine.

VII

EXULTATION is the going
Of an inland soul to sea, —
Past the houses, past the headlands,
Into deep eternity!

Bred as we, among the mountains,
Can the sailor understand
The divine intoxication
Of the first league out from land?

---

*Solve, as a problem.
†Clue.

VIII

Look back on time with kindly eyes,
He doubtless did his best;
How softly sinks his trembling sun
In human nature's west!

IX

A train went through a burial gate,
A bird broke forth and sang,
And trilled, and quivered, and shook his throat
Till all the churchyard rang;

And then adjusted his little notes,
And bowed and sang again.
Doubtless, he thought it meet of him
To say good-by to men.

X

I died for beauty, but was scarce
Adjusted in the tomb,
When one who died for truth was lain
In an adjoining room.

He questioned softly why I failed?
"For beauty," I replied.
"And I for truth, — the two are one;
We brethren are," he said.

And so, as kinsmen met a night,
We talked between the rooms,
Until the moss had reached our lips,
And covered up our names.

XI

How many times these low feet staggered,
Only the soldered mouth can tell;
Try! can you stir the awful rivet?
Try! can you lift the hasps* of steel?

Stroke the cool forehead, hot so often,
Lift, if you can, the listless hair;
Handle the adamantine† fingers
Never a thimble more shall wear.

Buzz the dull flies on the chamber window;
Brave shines the sun through the freckled pane;
Fearless the cobweb swings from the ceiling—
Indolent housewife, in daisies lain!

XII

I like a look of agony,
Because I know it's true;
Men do not sham convulsion,
Nor simulate a throe.

---

*Metal fasteners.
†Unyielding, like the hard precious stone adamant.

The eyes glaze once, and that is death.
Impossible to feign
The beads upon the forehead
By homely anguish strung.

XIII

THAT short, potential stir
That each can make but once,
That bustle so illustrious
'T is almost consequence,

Is the *éclat** of death.
Oh, thou unknown renown
That not a beggar would accept,
Had he the power to spurn!

XIV

I went to thank her,
But she slept;
Her bed a funnelled stone,
With nosegays† at the head and foot,
That travellers had thrown,

Who went to thank her;
But she slept.
'T was short to cross the sea

---

*Brilliant display, as in a performance.
†Small bunches of flowers.

To look upon her like, alive,
But turning back 't was slow.

XV

I'VE seen a dying eye
Run round and round a room
In search of something, as it seemed,
Then cloudier become;
And then, obscure with fog,
And then be soldered down,
Without disclosing what it be,
'T were blessed to have seen.

XVI

THE clouds their backs together laid,
The north begun to push,
The forests galloped till they fell,
The lightning skipped like mice;
The thunder crumbled like a stuff—
How good to be safe in tombs,
Where nature's temper cannot reach,
Nor vengeance ever comes!

XVII

I never saw a moor,
I never saw the sea;

Yet know I how the heather* looks,
And what a wave must be.

I never spoke with God,
Nor visited in heaven;
Yet certain am I of the spot
As if the chart were given.

XVIII

GOD permits industrious angels
Afternoons to play.
I met one,—forgot my school-mates,
All, for him, straightway.

God calls home the angels promptly
At the setting sun;
I missed mine. How dreary marbles,
After playing Crown!

XIX

To know just how he suffered would be dear;
To know if any human eyes were near
To whom he could intrust his wavering gaze,
Until it settled firm on Paradise.

To know if he was patient, part content,
Was dying as he thought, or different;

---

*Low-growing shrub with small, usually pinkish-purple flowers, which grows abundantly on moors.

Was it a pleasant day to die,
And did the sunshine face his way?

What was his furthest mind, of home, or God,
Or what the distant say
At news that he ceased human nature
On such a day?

And wishes, had he any?
Just his sigh, accented,
Had been legible to me.
And was he confident until
Ill fluttered out in everlasting well?

And if he spoke, what name was best,
What first,
What one broke off with
At the drowsiest?

Was he afraid, or tranquil?
Might he know
How conscious consciousness could grow,
Till love that was, and love too blest to be,
Meet—and the junction be Eternity?

XX

THE last night that she lived,
It was a common night,
Except the dying; this to us
Made nature different.

We noticed smallest things,—
Things overlooked before,

By this great light upon our minds
Italicized, as 't were.

That others could exist
While she must finish quite,
A jealousy for her arose
So nearly infinite.

We waited while she passed;
It was a narrow time,
Too jostled were our souls to speak,
At length the notice came.

She mentioned, and forgot;
Then lightly as a reed
Bent to the water, shivered scarce,
Consented, and was dead.

And we, we placed the hair,
And drew the head erect;
And then an awful leisure was,
Our faith to regulate.

XXI

NOT in this world to see his face
Sounds long, until I read the place
Where this is said to be
But just the primer to a life
Unopened, rare, upon the shelf,
Clasped yet to him and me.

And yet, my primer suits me so
I would not choose a book to know
Than that, be sweeter wise;

Might some one else so learned be,
And leave me just my A B C,
Himself could have the skies.

XXII

THE bustle in a house
The morning after death
Is solemnest of industries
Enacted upon earth, —

The sweeping up the heart,
And putting love away
We shall not want to use again
Until eternity.

XXIII

I reason, earth is short,
And anguish absolute.
And many hurt;
But what of that?

I reason, we could die:
The best vitality
Cannot excel decay;
But what of that?

I reason that in heaven
Somehow, it will be even,
Some new equation given;
But what of that?

XXIV

AFRAID? Of whom am I afraid?
Not death; for who is he?
The porter of my father's lodge
As much abasheth* me.

Of life? 'T were odd I fear a thing
That comprehendeth† me
In one or more existences
At Deity's decree.

Of resurrection? Is the east
Afraid to trust the morn
With her fastidious forehead?
As soon impeach my crown!

XXV

THE sun kept setting, setting still;
No hue of afternoon
Upon the village I perceived,—
From house to house 't was noon.

The dusk kept dropping, dropping still;
No dew upon the grass,
But only on my forehead stopped,
And wandered in my face.

My feet kept drowsing, drowsing still,
My fingers were awake;

---

*Abashes, disconcerts.
†Includes.

Yet why so little sound myself
Unto my seeming make?

How well I knew the light before!
I could not see it now.
'T is dying, I am doing; but
I'm not afraid to know.

XXVI

Two swimmers wrestled on the spar*
Until the morning sun,
When one turned smiling to the land.
O God, the other one!

The stray ships passing spied a face
Upon the waters borne,
With eyes in death still begging raised,
And hands beseeching thrown.

XXVII

BECAUSE I could not stop for Death,
He kindly stopped for me;
The carriage held but just ourselves
And Immortality.

We slowly drove, he knew no haste,
And I had put away

---

*The biblical story of Jacob wrestling the angel (see the Bible, Genesis 32:24–30)
seems to inform this poem; a spar is a stout pole used to support sails and rigging.

My labor, and my leisure too,
For his civility.

We passed the school where children played
At wrestling in a ring;
We passed the fields of gazing grain,
We passed the setting sun.

We paused before a house that seemed
A swelling of the ground;
The roof was scarcely visible,
The cornice* but a mound.

Since then 't is centuries; but each
Feels shorter than the day
I first surmised the horses' heads
Were toward eternity.

XXVIII

SHE went as quiet as the dew
From a familiar flower.
Not like the dew did she return
At the accustomed hour!

She dropt as softly as a star
From out my summer's eve;
Less skillful than Leverrier†
It's sorer to believe!

---

*Horizontal molded crown atop a building or wall.
†Urbain-Jean-Joseph Leverrier (1811–1877), a French astronomer who discovered
evidence of the planet Neptune.

XXIX

At last to be identified!
At last, the lamps upon thy side,
The rest of life to see!
Past midnight, past the morning star!
Past sunrise! Ah! what leagues there are
Between our feet and day!

XXX

Except to heaven, she is nought;
Except for angels, lone;
Except to some wide-wandering bee,
A flower superfluous blown;

Except for winds, provincial;
Except by butterflies,
Unnoticed as a single dew
That on the acre lies.

The smallest housewife in the grass,
Yet take her from the lawn,
And somebody has lost the face
That made existence home!

XXXI

Death is a dialogue between
The spirit and the dust.

"Dissolve," says Death. The Spirit, "Sir,
I have another trust."

Death doubts it, argues from the ground.
The Spirit turns away,
Just laying off, for evidence,
An overcoat of clay.

XXXII

IT was too late for man,
But early yet for God;
Creation impotent to help,
But prayer remained our side.

How excellent the heaven,
When earth cannot be had;
How hospitable, then, the face
Of our old neighbor, God!

XXXIII*

WHEN I was small, a woman died.
To-day her only boy
Went up from the Potomac,
His face all victory,

---

*Thomas H. Johnson, editor of *The Complete Poems of Emily Dickinson* (see For Further Reading) dates this poem from 1862; perhaps Dickinson is commenting on the Civil War.

To look at her; how slowly
The seasons must have turned
Till bullets clipt* an angle,
And he passed quickly round!

If pride shall be in Paradise
I never can decide;
Of their imperial conduct,
No person testified.

But proud in apparition,
That woman and her boy
Pass back and forth before my brain,
As ever in the sky.

XXXIV

THE daisy follows soft the sun,
And when his golden walk is done,
    Sits shyly at his feet.
He, waking, finds the flower near.
"Wherefore, marauder, art thou here?"
    "Because, sir, love is sweet!"

We are the flower, Thou the sun!
Forgive us, if as days decline,
    We nearer steal to Thee,—
Enamoured of the parting west,
The peace, the flight, the amethyst,
    Night's possibility!

*Cut off, shortened.

XXXV

No rack can torture me,
My soul's at liberty.
Behind this mortal bone
There knits a bolder one

You cannot prick with saw,
Nor rend with scymitar.*
Two bodies therefore be;
Bind one, and one will flee.

The eagle of his nest
No easier divest
And gain the sky,
Than mayest thou,

Except thyself may be
Thine enemy;
Captivity is consciousness,
So's liberty.

XXXVI

I lost a world the other day.
Has anybody found?
You'll know it by the row of stars
Around its forehead bound.

A rich man might not notice it;
Yet to my frugal eye

---

*Scimitar; a curved sword.

Of more esteem than ducats.*
Oh, find it, sir, for me!

XXXVII

If I shouldn't be alive
When the robins come,
Give the one in red cravat†
A memorial crumb.

If I couldn't thank you,
Being just asleep,
You will know I'm trying
With my granite lip!

XXXVIII

Sleep is supposed to be,
By souls of sanity,
The shutting of the eye.

Sleep is the station grand
Down which on either hand
The hosts of witness stand!

Morn is supposed to be,
By people of degree,
The breaking of the day.

---

*Gold coins once used as currency in some European countries.
†Scarf worn around the neck; necktie.

Morning has not occurred!
That shall aurora be
East of eternity;

One with the banner gay,
One in the red array, —
That is the break of day.

XXXIX

I shall know why, when time is over,
And I have ceased to wonder why;
Christ will explain each separate anguish
In the fair schoolroom of the sky.

He will tell me what Peter* promised,
And I, for wonder at his woe,
I shall forget the drop of anguish
That scalds me now, that scalds me now.

XL

I never lost as much but twice,
And that was in the sod;
Twice have I stood a beggar
Before the door of God!

Angels, twice descending,
Reimbursed my store.

---

*Chief of the twelve Apostles; traditionally regarded as the first bishop of Rome.

Burglar, banker, father,
I am poor once more!

XLI

LET down the bars, O Death!
The tired flocks come in
Whose bleating ceases to repeat,
Whose wandering is done.

Thine is the stillest night,
Thine the securest fold;*
Too near thou art for seeking thee,
Too tender to be told.

XLII

GOING to heaven!
I don't know when,
Pray do not ask me how, —
Indeed, I'm too astonished
To think of answering you!
Going to heaven! —
How dim it sounds!
And yet it will be done
As sure as flocks go home at night
Unto the shepherd's arm!

Perhaps you're going too!
Who knows?

---

*Flock of sheep.

If you should get there first,
Save just a little place for me
Close to the two I lost!
The smallest "robe" will fit me,
And just a bit of "crown";
For you know we do not mind our dress
When we are going home.

I'm glad I don't believe it,
For it would stop my breath,
And I'd like to look a little more
At such a curious earth!
I am glad they did believe it
Whom I have never found
Since the mighty autumn afternoon
I left them in the ground.

XLIII

At least to pray is left, is left.
O Jesus! in the air
I know not which thy chamber is, —
I'm knocking everywhere.

Thou stirrest earthquake in the South,
And maelstrom in the sea;
Say, Jesus Christ of Nazareth,
Hast thou no arm for me?

XLIV

Step lightly on this narrow spot!
The broadest land that grows

Is not so ample as the breast
These emerald seams enclose.

Step lofty; for this name is told
As far as cannon dwell,
Or flag subsist, or fame export
Her deathless syllable.

XLV

Morns like these we parted;
Noons like these she rose,
Fluttering first, then firmer,
To her fair repose.

Never did she lisp it,
And 't was not for me;
She was mute from transport,
I, from agony!

Till the evening, nearing,
One the shutters drew —
Quick! a sharper rustling!
And this linnet* flew!

XLVI

A death-blow is a life-blow to some
Who, till they died, did not alive become;

*Small, brownish finch.

Who, had they lived, had died, but when
They died, vitality begun.

XLVII

I read my sentence steadily,
Reviewed it with my eyes,
To see that I made no mistake
In its extremest clause, —

The date, and manner of the shame;
And then the pious form
That "God have mercy"* on the soul
The jury voted him.

I made my soul familiar
With her extremity,
That at the last it should not be
A novel agony,

But she and Death, acquainted,
Meet tranquilly as friends,
Salute and pass without a hint —
And there the matter ends.

XLVIII

I have not told my garden yet,
Lest that should conquer me;

---

*Quote from "The Jesus Prayer": "Lord Jesus Christ, Son of God, have mercy on
me, a sinner."

I have not quite the strength now
To break it to the bee.

I will not name it in the street,
For shops would stare, that I,
So shy, so very ignorant,
Should have the face to die.

The hillsides must not know it,
Where I have rambled so,
Nor tell the loving forests
The day that I shall go,

Nor lisp it at the table,
Nor heedless by the way
Hint that within the riddle
One will walk to-day!

XLIX

THEY dropped like flakes, they dropped like stars,
    Like petals from a rose,
When suddenly across the June
    A wind with fingers goes.

They perished in the seamless grass,—
    No eye could find the place;
But God on his repealless* list
    Can summon every face.

---

*Irrevocable.

L

THE only ghost I ever saw
Was dressed in mechlin,* — so;
He wore no sandal on his foot,
And stepped like flakes of snow.
His gait was soundless, like the bird,
But rapid, like the roe;
His fashions quaint, mosaic,†
Or, haply, mistletoe.

His conversation seldom,
His laughter like the breeze
That dies away in dimples
Among the pensive trees.
Our interview was transient, —
Of me, himself was shy;
And God forbid I look behind
Since that appalling day!

LI

SOME, too fragile for winter winds,
The thoughtful grave encloses, —
Tenderly tucking them in from frost
Before their feet are cold.

Never the treasures in her nest
The cautious grave exposes,
Building where schoolboy dare not look
And sportsman is not bold.

---

*Delicate lace.
†Relating to Moses, the Hebrew prophet who led the Israelites out of Egypt.

This covert* have all the children
Early aged, and often cold, —
Sparrows unnoticed by the Father;
Lambs for whom time had not a fold.

LII

As by the dead we love to sit,
Become so wondrous dear,
As for the lost we grapple,
Though all the rest are here, —

In broken mathematics
We estimate our prize,
Vast, in its fading ratio,
To our penurious eyes!

LIII

DEATH sets a thing significant
The eye had hurried by,
Except a perished creature
Entreat us tenderly

To ponder little workmanships
In crayon or in wool,
With "This was last her fingers did,"
Industrious until

---

*Covered shelter; hiding place.

The thimble weighed too heavy,
The stitches stopped themselves,
And then 't was put among the dust
Upon the closet shelves.

A book I have, a friend gave,
Whose pencil, here and there,
Had notched the place that pleased him, —
At rest his fingers are.

Now, when I read, I read not,
For interrupting tears
Obliterate the etchings
Too costly for repairs.

LIV

I went to heaven, —
'T was a small town,
Lit with a ruby,
Lathed* with down.
Stiller than the fields
At the full dew,
Beautiful as pictures
No man drew.
People like the moth,
Of mechlin, frames,
Duties of gossamer,
And eider† names.
Almost contented
I could be

---

*Spread.
†Down of an eider duck.

'Mong such unique
Society.

LV

THEIR height in heaven comforts not,
Their glory nought to me;
'T was best imperfect, as it was;
I'm finite, I can't see.

The house of supposition,
The glimmering frontier
That skirts the acres of perhaps,
To me shows insecure.

The wealth I had contented me;
If 't was a meaner size,
Then I had counted it until
It pleased my narrow eyes

Better than larger values,
However true their show;
This timid life of evidence
Keeps pleading, "I don't know."

LVI

THERE is a shame of nobleness
Confronting sudden pelf, — *

---

*Wealth or riches, especially when dishonestly acquired.

A finer shame of ecstasy
Convicted of itself.

A best disgrace a brave man feels,
Acknowledged of the brave, —
One more "Ye Blessed" to be told;
But this involves the grave.

LVII

A triumph may be of several kinds.
There's triumph in the room
When that old imperator,* Death,
By faith is overcome.

There's triumph of the finer mind
When truth, affronted long,
Advances calm to her supreme,
Her God her only throng.

A triumph when temptation's bribe
Is slowly handed back,
One eye upon the heaven renounced
And one upon the rack.

Severer triumph, by himself
Experienced, who can pass
Acquitted from that naked bar,
Jehovah's countenance!

---

*Army commander in the ancient Roman Republic.

LVIII

POMPLESS no life can pass away;
        The lowliest career
To the same pageant wends* its way
        As that exalted here.
How cordial is the mystery!
        The hospitable pall
A "this way" beckons spaciously, —
        A miracle for all!

LIX

I noticed people disappeared,
When but a little child, —
Supposed they visited remote,
Or settled regions wild.

Now know I they both visited
And settled regions wild,
But did because they died, — a fact
Withheld the little child!

LX

I had no cause to be awake,
My best was gone to sleep,
And morn a new politeness took
And failed to wake them up,

---

*Proceeds.

But called the others clear,
And passed their curtains by.
Sweet morning, when I over-sleep,
Knock, recollect, for me!

I looked at sunrise once,
And then I looked at them,
And wishfulness in me arose
For circumstance the same.

'T was such an ample peace,
It could not hold a sigh, —
'T was Sabbath with the bells divorced,
'T was sunset all the day.

So choosing but a gown
And taking but a prayer,
The only raiment I should need,
I struggled, and was there.

LXI

IF anybody's friend be dead,
It's sharpest of the theme
The thinking how they walked alive,
At such and such a time.

Their costume, of a Sunday,
Some manner of the hair, —
A prank nobody knew but them,
Lost, in the sepulchre.

How warm they were on such a day:
You almost feel the date,

So short way off it seems; and now,
They're centuries from that.

How pleased they were at what you said;
You try to touch the smile,
And dip your fingers in the frost:
When was it, can you tell,

You asked the company to tea,
Acquaintance, just a few,
And chatted close with this grand thing
That don't remember you?

Past bows and invitations,
Past interview, and vow,
Past what ourselves can estimate,—
That makes the quick of woe!

LXII

Our journey had advanced;
Our feet were almost come
To that odd fork in Being's road,
Eternity by term.

Our pace took sudden awe,
Our feet reluctant led.
Before were cities, but between,
The forest of the dead.

Retreat was out of hope,—
Behind, a sealed route,
Eternity's white flag before,
And God at every gate.

LXIII

AMPLE make this bed.
Make this bed with awe;
In it wait till judgment break
Excellent and fair.

Be its mattress straight,
Be its pillow round;
Let no sunrise' yellow noise
Interrupt this ground.

LXIV

ON such a night, or such a night,
Would anybody care
If such a little figure
Slipped quiet from its chair,

So quiet, oh, how quiet!
That nobody might know
But that the little figure
Rocked softer, to and fro?

On such a dawn, or such a dawn,
Would anybody sigh
That such a little figure
Too sound asleep did lie

For chanticleer to wake it, —
Or stirring house below,
Or giddy bird in orchard,
Or early task to do?

There was a little figure plump
For every little knoll,
Busy needles, and spools of thread,
And trudging feet from school.

Playmates, and holidays, and nuts,
And visions vast and small.
Strange that the feet so precious charged
Should reach so small a goal!

LXV

ESSENTIAL oils are wrung:
The attar from the rose
Is not expressed by suns alone,
It is the gift of screws.

The general rose decays;
But this, in lady's drawer,
Makes summer when the lady lies
In ceaseless rosemary.

LXVI

I lived on dread; to those who know
The stimulus there is
In danger, other impetus
Is numb and vital-less.*

---

*Lifeless.

As 't were a spur upon the soul,
A fear will urge it where
To go without the spectre's aid
Were challenging despair.

LXVII

If I should die,
And you should live,
And time should gurgle on,
And morn should beam,
And noon should burn,
As it has usual done;
If birds should build as early,
And bees as bustling go, —
One might depart at option
From enterprise below!
'T is sweet to know that stocks will stand
When we with daisies lie,
That commerce will continue,
And trades as briskly fly.
It makes the parting tranquil
And keeps the soul serene,
That gentlemen so sprightly
Conduct the pleasing scene!

LXVIII

Her final summer was it,
And yet we guessed it not;

If tenderer industriousness
Pervaded her, we thought

A further force of life
Developed from within,—
When Death lit all the shortness up,
And made the hurry plain.

We wondered at our blindness,—
When nothing was to see
But her Carrara* guide-post,—
At our stupidity,

When, duller than our dulness,
The busy darling lay,
So busy was she, finishing,
So leisurely were we!

LXIX

ONE need not be a chamber to be haunted,
One need not be a house;
The brain has corridors surpassing
Material place.

Far safer, of a midnight meeting
External ghost,
Than an interior confronting
That whiter host.

Far safer through an Abbey gallop,
The stones achase,†

---

*Town of northern Italy known for its marble quarries.
†In pursuit.

Than, moonless, one's own self encounter
In lonesome place.

Ourself, behind ourself concealed,
Should startle most;
Assassin, hid in our apartment,
Be horror's least.

The prudent carries a revolver,
He bolts the door,
O'erlooking a superior spectre
More near.

LXX

She died, — this was the way she died;
And when her breath was done,
Took up her simple wardrobe
And started for the sun.
Her little figure at the gate
The angels must have spied,
Since I could never find her
Upon the mortal side.

LXXI

Wait till the majesty of Death
Invests so mean a brow!
Almost a powdered footman
Might dare to touch it now!

Wait till in everlasting robes
This democrat is dressed,
Then prate about "preferment"
And "station" and the rest!

Around this quiet courtier
Obsequious angels wait!
Full royal is his retinue,
Full purple is his state!

A lord might dare to lift the hat
To such a modest clay,
Since that my Lord, "the Lord of lords"
Receives unblushingly!

LXXII

WENT up a year this evening!
I recollect it well!
Amid no bells nor bravos
The bystanders will tell!
Cheerful, as to the village,
Tranquil, as to repose,
Chastened, as to the chapel,
This humble tourist rose.
Did not talk of returning,
Alluded to no time
When, were the gales propitious,
We might look for him;
Was grateful for the roses
In life's diverse bouquet,
Talked softly of new species
To pick another day.
Beguiling thus the wonder,
The wondrous nearer drew;

Hands bustled at the moorings—
The crowd respectful grew.
Ascended from our vision
To countenances new!
A difference, a daisy,
Is all the rest I knew!

LXXIII

TAKEN from men this morning,
Carried by men to-day,
Met by the gods with banners
Who marshalled her away.

One little maid from playmates,
One little mind from school,—
There must be guests in Eden;
All the rooms are full.

Far as the east from even,
Dim as the border star,—
Courtiers quaint, in kingdoms,
Our departed are.

LXXIV

WHAT inn is this
Where for the night
Peculiar traveller comes?
Who is the landlord?
Where the maids?
Behold, what curious rooms!

No ruddy fires on the hearth,
No brimming tankards flow.
Necromancer, landlord,
Who are these below?

LXXV

It was not death, for I stood up,
And all the dead lie down;
It was not night, for all the bells
Put out their tongues, for noon.

It was not frost, for on my flesh
I felt siroccos* crawl, —
Nor fire, for just my marble feet
Could keep a chancel† cool.

And yet it tasted like them all;
The figures I have seen
Set orderly, for burial,
Reminded me of mine,

As if my life were shaven
And fitted to a frame,
And could not breathe without a key;
And 't was like midnight, some,

When everything that ticked has stopped,
And space stares, all around,
Or grisly frosts, first autumn morns,
Repeal the beating ground.

---

*Hot southerly winds.
†Area in a church containing the altar and seating for clergy and choir.

But most like chaos,—stopless, cool,—
Without a chance or spar,
Or even a report of land
To justify despair.

LXXVI

I should not dare to leave my friend,
Because—because if he should die
While I was gone, and I—too late—
Should reach the heart that wanted me;

If I should disappoint the eyes
That hunted, hunted so, to see,
And could not bear to shut until
They "noticed" me—they noticed me;

If I should stab the patient faith
So sure I'd come—so sure I'd come,
It listening, listening, went to sleep
Telling my tardy name,—

My heart would wish it broke before,
Since breaking then, since breaking then,
Were useless as next morning's sun,
Where midnight frosts had lain!

LXXVII

GREAT streets of silence led away
To neighborhoods of pause;

Here was no notice, no dissent,
No universe, no laws.

By clocks 't was morning, and for night
The bells at distance called;
But epoch had no basis here,
For period exhaled.

LXXVIII

A throe upon the features
A hurry in the breath,
An ecstasy of parting
Denominated "Death", —

An anguish at the mention,
Which, when to patience grown,
I've known permission given
To rejoin its own.

LXXIX

Of tribulation these are they
Denoted by the white;
The spangled gowns, a lesser rank
Of victors designate.

All these did conquer; but the ones
Who overcame most times
Wear nothing commoner than snow,
No ornament but palms.

Surrender is a sort unknown
On this superior soil;
Defeat, an outgrown anguish,
Remembered as the mile

Our panting ankle barely gained
When night devoured the road;
But we stood whispering in the house,
And all we said was "Saved!"

LXXX

I think just how my shape will rise
When I shall be forgiven,
Till hair and eyes and timid head
Are out of sight, in heaven.

I think just how my lips will weigh
With shapeless, quivering prayer
That you, so late, consider me,
The sparrow of your care.

I mind me that of anguish sent,
Some drifts were moved away
Before my simple bosom broke,—
And why not this, if they?

And so, until delirious borne
I con* that thing,—"forgiven,"—
Till with long fright and longer trust
I drop my heart, unshriven!†

---

*Study or examine carefully; memorize.
†Unabsolved (as by a confession).

LXXXI

AFTER a hundred years
Nobody knows the place,—
Agony, that enacted there,
Motionless as peace.

Weeds triumphant ranged,
Strangers strolled and spelled
At the lone orthography*
Of the elder dead.

Winds of summer fields
Recollect the way,—
Instinct picking up the key
Dropped by memory.

LXXXII

LAY this laurel on the one
Too intrinsic for renown.
Laurel! veil your deathless tree,—
Him you chasten, that is he!

LXXXIII

THIS world is not conclusion;
    A sequel stands beyond,
Invisible, as music,

---

*Art or study of standard spelling.

But positive, as sound.
It beckons and it baffles;
    Philosophies don't know,
And through a riddle, at the last,
    Sagacity must go.
To guess it puzzles scholars;
    To gain it, men have shown
Contempt of generations,
    And crucifixion known.

LXXXIV

WE learn in the retreating
    How vast an one
Was recently among us.
    A perished sun

Endears in the departure
    How doubly more
Than all the golden presence
    It was before!

LXXXV

THEY say that "time assuages," —
    Time never did assuage;
An actual suffering strengthens,
    As sinews do, with age.

Time is a test of trouble,
    But not a remedy.

If such it prove, it prove too
There was no malady.

LXXXVI

WE cover thee, sweet face.
    Not that we tire of thee,
But that thyself fatigue of us;
    Remember, as thou flee,
We follow thee until
    Thou notice us no more,
And then, reluctant, turn away
    To con thee o'er and o'er,
And blame the scanty love
    We were content to show,
Augmented, sweet, a hundred fold
    If thou would'st take it now.

LXXXVII

THAT is solemn we have ended, —
    Be it but a play,
Or a glee* among the garrets,
    Or a holiday,

Or a leaving home; or later,
    Parting with a world
We have understood, for better
    Still it be unfurled.

---

*Unaccompanied part-song for three or more male voices, popular in the eighteenth century.

LXXXVIII

THE stimulus, beyond the grave
    His countenance to see,
Supports me like imperial drams
    Afforded royally.

LXXXIX

GIVEN in marriage unto thee,
    Oh, thou celestial host!
Bride of the Father and the Son,
    Bride of the Holy Ghost!

Other betrothal shall dissolve,
    Wedlock of will decay;
Only the keeper of this seal
    Conquers mortality.

XC

THAT such have died enables us
    The tranquiller to die;
That such have lived, certificate
    For immortality.

XCI

THEY won't frown always, — some sweet day
    When I forget to tease,

They'll recollect how cold I looked,
    And how I just said "please."

Then they will hasten to the door
    To call the little child,
Who cannot thank them, for the ice
    That on her lisping piled.

XCII

'T is an honorable thought,
    And makes one lift one's hat,
As one encountered gentlefolk
    Upon a daily street,

That we've immortal place,
    Though pyramids decay,
And kingdoms, like the orchard,
    Flit russetly away.

XCIII

THE distance that the dead have gone
    Does not at first appear;
Their coming back seems possible
    For many an ardent year.

And then, that we have followed them
    We more than half suspect,
So intimate have we become
    With their dear retrospect.

XCIV

How dare the robins sing,
    When men and women hear
Who since they went to their account
    Have settled with the year! —
Paid all that life had earned
    In one consummate bill,
And now, what life or death can do
    Is immaterial.
Insulting is the sun
    To him whose mortal light,
Beguiled of immortality,
    Bequeaths him to the night.
In deference to him
    Extinct be every hum,
Whose garden wrestles with the dew,
    At daybreak overcome!

XCV

DEATH is like the insect
    Menacing the tree,
Competent to kill it,
    But decoyed* may be.

Bait it with the balsam,†
    Seek it with the knife,
Baffle, if it cost you
    Everything in life.

---

*Lured away.
†Oily aromatic resin from plants.

Then, if it have burrowed
    Out of reach of skill,
Ring the tree and leave it, —
    'T is the vermin's will.

XCVI

'T is sunrise, little maid, hast thou
    No station in the day?
'T was not thy wont to hinder so, —
Retrieve thine industry.

'T is noon, my little maid, alas!
    And art thou sleeping yet?
The lily waiting to be wed,
    The bee, dost thou forget?

My little maid, 't is night; alas,
    That night should be to thee
Instead of morning! Hadst thou broached
    Thy little plan to me,
Dissuade thee if I could not, sweet,
    I might have aided thee.

XCVII

EACH that we lose takes part of us;
A crescent still abides,
Which like the moon, some turbid night,
Is summoned by the tides.

XCVIII

Not any higher stands the grave
        For heroes than for men;
Not any nearer for the child
        Than numb three-score and ten.*

This latest leisure equal lulls
        The beggar and his queen;
Propitiate this democrat
        By summer's gracious mien.†

XCIX

As far from pity as complaint,
        As cool to speech as stone,
As numb to revelation
        As if my trade were bone.

As far from time as history,
        As near yourself to-day
As children to the rainbow's scarf,
        Or sunset's yellow play

To eyelids in the sepulchre.
        How still the dancer lies,
While color's revelations break,
        And blaze the butterflies!

---

*Seventy (a score is equivalent to twenty).
†Bearing or manner.

C

'T is whiter than an Indian pipe,
    'T is dimmer than a lace;
No stature has it, like a fog,
    When you approach the place.

Not any voice denotes it here,
    Or intimates it there;
A spirit, how doth it accost?
    What customs hath the air?

This limitless hyperbole
    Each one of us shall be;
'T is drama, if (hypothesis)
    It be not tragedy!

CI

SHE laid her docile crescent down,
    And this mechanic stone
Still states, to dates that have forgot,
    The news that she is gone.

So constant to its stolid trust,
    The shaft that never knew,
It shames the constancy that fled
    Before its emblem flew.

CII

BLESS God, he went as soldiers,
    His musket on his breast;

Grant, God, he charge the bravest
    Of all the martial blest.

Please God, might I behold him
    In epauletted white,
I should not fear the foe then,
    I should not fear the fight.

CIII

IMMORTAL is an ample word
    When what we need is by,
But when it leaves us for a time,
    'T is a necessity.

Of heaven above the firmest proof
    We fundamental know,
Except for its marauding hand,
    It had been heaven below.

CIV

WHERE every bird is bold to go,
    And bees abashless play,
The foreigner before he knocks
    Must thrust the tears away.

CV

THE grave my little cottage is,
    Where, keeping house for thee,

I make my parlor orderly,
      And lay the marble tea,

For two divided, briefly,
      A cycle, it may be,
Till everlasting life unite
      In strong society.

CVI

THIS was in the white of the year,
      That was in the green,
Drifts were as difficult then to think
      As daisies now to be seen.

Looking back is best that is left,
      Or if it be before,
Retrospection is prospect's half,
      Sometimes almost more.

CVII

SWEET hours have perished here;
      This is a mighty room;
Within its precincts hopes have played, —
      Now shadows in the tomb.

CVIII

ME! Come! My dazzled face
In such a shining place!

Me! Hear! My foreign ear
The sounds of welcome near!

The saints shall meet
Our bashful feet.

My holiday shall be
That they remember me;

My paradise, the fame
That they pronounce my name.

CIX

From us she wandered now a year,
　　Her tarrying unknown;
If wilderness prevent her feet,
　　Or that ethereal zone

No eye hath seen and lived,
　　We ignorant must be.
We only know what time of year
　　We took the mystery.

CX

I wish I knew that woman's name,
　　So, when she comes this way,
To hold my life, and hold my ears,
　　For fear I hear her say

She's "sorry I am dead", again,
　　Just when the grave and I
Have sobbed ourselves almost to sleep,—
　　Our only lullaby.

CXI

Bereaved of all, I went abroad,
　　No less bereaved to be
Upon a new peninsula,—
　　The grave preceded me,

Obtained my lodgings ere myself,
　　And when I sought my bed,
The grave it was, reposed upon
　　The pillow for my head.

I waked, to find it first awake,
　　I rose,—it followed me;
I tried to drop it in the crowd,
　　To lose it in the sea,

In cups of artificial drowse
　　To sleep its shape away,—
The grave was finished, but the spade
　　Remained in memory.

CXII

I felt a funeral in my brain,
　　And mourners, to and fro,

Kept treading, treading, till it seemed
     That sense was breaking through.

And when they all were seated,
     A service like a drum
Kept beating, beating, till I thought
     My mind was going numb.

And then I heard them lift a box,
     And creak across my soul
With those same boots of lead, again.
     Then space began to toll

As all the heavens were a bell,
     And Being but an ear,
And I and silence some strange race,
     Wrecked, solitary, here.

CXIII

I meant to find her when I came;
     Death had the same design;
But the success was his, it seems,
     And the discomfit mine.

I meant to tell her how I longed
     For just this single time;
But Death had told her so the first,
     And she had hearkened him.

To wander now is my abode;
     To rest, — to rest would be
A privilege of hurricane
     To memory and me.

CXIV

I sing to use the waiting,
    My bonnet but to tie,
And shut the door unto my house;
    No more to do have I,

Till, his best step approaching,
    We journey to the day,
And tell each other how we sang
    To keep the dark away.

CXV

A sickness of this world it most occasions
    When best men die;
A wishfulness their far condition
    To occupy.

A chief indifference, as foreign
    A world must be
Themselves forsake contented,
    For Deity.

CXVI

SUPERFLUOUS were the sun
    When excellence is dead;
He were superfluous every day,
    For every day is said

That syllable whose faith
   Just saves it from despair,
And whose "I'll meet you" hesitates —
   If love inquire, "Where?"

Upon his dateless fame
   Our periods may lie,
As stars that drop anonymous
   From an abundant sky.

CXVII

So proud she was to die
   It made us all ashamed
That what we cherished, so unknown
   To her desire seemed.

So satisfied to go
   Where none of us should be,
Immediately, that anguish stooped
   Almost to jealousy.

CXVIII

TIE the strings to my life, my Lord,
   Then I am ready to go!
Just a look at the horses —
   Rapid! That will do!

Put me in on the firmest side,
   So I shall never fall;

For we must ride to the Judgment,
    And it's partly down hill.

But never I mind the bridges,
    And never I mind the sea;
Held fast in everlasting race
    By my own choice and thee.

Good-by to the life I used to live,
    And the world I used to know;
And kiss the hills for me, just once;
    Now I am ready to go!

CXIX

THE dying need but little, dear, —
    A glass of water's all,
A flower's unobtrusive face
    To punctuate the wall,

A fan, perhaps, a friend's regret,
    And certainly that one
No color in the rainbow
    Perceives when you are gone.

CXX

THERE'S something quieter than sleep
    Within this inner room!
It wears a sprig upon its breast,
    And will not tell its name.

Some touch it and some kiss it,
    Some chafe its idle hand;
It has a simple gravity
    I do not understand!

While simple-hearted neighbors
    Chat of the "early dead",
We, prone to periphrasis,*
    Remark that birds have fled!

CXXI

THE soul should always stand ajar,
    That if the heaven inquire,
He will not be obliged to wait,
    Or shy of troubling her.

Depart, before the host has slid
    The bolt upon the door,
To seek for the accomplished guest—
    Her visitor no more.

CXXII

THREE weeks passed since I had seen her,—
    Some disease had vexed;
'T was with text and village singing
    I beheld her next,

---

*Circumlocution, or long-winded speech.

And a company—our pleasure
    To discourse alone;
Gracious now to me as any,
    Gracious unto none.

Borne, without dissent of either,
    To the parish night;
Of the separated people
    Which are out of sight?

CXXIII

I breathed enough to learn the trick,
    And now, removed from air,
I simulate the breath so well,
    That one, to be quite sure

The lungs are stirless, must descend
    Among the cunning cells,
And touch the pantomime himself.
    How cool the bellows feels!

CXXIV

I wonder if the sepulchre
    Is not a lonesome way,
When men and boys, and larks and June
    Go down the fields to hay!

CXXV

IF tolling bell I ask the cause.
    "A soul has gone to God,"
I'm answered in a lonesome tone;
    Is heaven then so sad?

That bells should joyful ring to tell
    A soul had gone to heaven,
Would seem to me the proper way
    A good news should be given.

CXXVI

IF I may have it when it's dead
    I will contented be;
If just as soon as breath is out
    It shall belong to me,

Until they lock it in the grave,
    'T is bliss I cannot weigh,
For though they lock thee in the grave,
    Myself can hold the key.

Think of it, lover! I and thee
    Permitted face to face to be;
After a life, a death we'll say, —
    For death was that, and this is thee.

CXXVII

BEFORE the ice is in the pools,
    Before the skaters go,

Or any cheek at nightfall
   Is tarnished by the snow,

Before the fields have finished,
   Before the Christmas tree,
Wonder upon wonder
   Will arrive to me!

What we touch the hems of
   On a summer's day;
What is only walking
   Just a bridge away;

That which sings so, speaks so,
   When there's no one here, —
Will the frock I wept in
   Answer me to wear?

CXXVIII

I heard a fly buzz when I died;
   The stillness round my form
Was like the stillness in the air
   Between the heaves of storm.

The eyes beside had wrung them dry,
   And breaths were gathering sure
For that last onset, when the king
   Be witnessed in his power.

I willed my keepsakes, signed away
   What portion of me I
Could make assignable, — and then
   There interposed a fly,

With blue, uncertain, stumbling buzz,
    Between the light and me;
And then the windows failed, and then
    I could not see to see.

CXXIX

ADRIFT! A little boat adrift!
    And night is coming down!
Will no one guide a little boat
    Unto the nearest town?

So sailors say, on yesterday,
    Just as the dusk was brown,
One little boat gave up its strife,
    And gurgled down and down.

But angels say, on yesterday,
    Just as the dawn was red,
One little boat o'erspent with gales
Retrimmed its masts, redecked its sails
    Exultant, onward sped!

CXXX

THERE'S been a death in the opposite house
    As lately as to-day.
I know it by the numb look
    Such houses have alway.*

---

*Always.

The neighbors rustle in and out,
    The doctor drives away.
A window opens like a pod,
    Abrupt, mechanically;

Somebody flings a mattress out,—
    The children hurry by;
They wonder if It died on that,—
    I used to when a boy.

The minister goes stiffly in
    As if the house were his,
And he owned all the mourners now,
    And little boys besides;

And then the milliner, and the man
    Of the appalling trade,
To take the measure of the house.
    There'll be that dark parade

Of tassels and of coaches soon;
    It's easy as a sign,—
The intuition of the news
    In just a country town.

CXXXI

WE never know we go,—when we are going
    We jest and shut the door;
Fate following behind us bolts it,
    And we accost no more.

CXXXII

It struck me every day
    The lightning was as new
As if the cloud that instant slit
    And let the fire through.

It burned me in the night,
    It blistered in my dream;
It sickened fresh upon my sight
    With every morning's beam.

I thought that storm was brief, —
    The maddest, quickest by;
But Nature lost the date of this,
    And left it in the sky.

CXXXIII

Water is taught by thirst;
Land, by the oceans passed;
    Transport, by throe;
Peace, by its battles told;
Love, by memorial mould;
    Birds, by the snow.

CXXXIV

We thirst at first, — 't is Nature's act;
    And later, when we die,

A little water supplicate
    Of fingers going by.

It intimates the finer want,
    Whose adequate supply
Is that great water in the west
    Termed immortality.

CXXXV

A clock stopped—not the mantel's;
    Geneva's farthest skill
Can't put the puppet bowing
    That just now dangled still.

An awe came on the trinket!
    The figures hunched with pain,
Then quivered out of decimals
    Into degreeless noon.

It will not stir for doctors,
    This pendulum of snow;
The shopman importunes it,
    While cool, concernless No

Nods from the gilded pointers,*
    Nods from the seconds slim,
Decades of arrogance between
    The dial life and him.

---

*Scale indicators on a clock.

CXXXVI

ALL overgrown by cunning moss,
　　All interspersed with weed,
The little cage of "Currer Bell",*
　　In quiet Haworth† laid.

This bird, observing others,
　　When frosts too sharp became,
Retire to other latitudes,
　　Quietly did the same.

But differed in returning;
　　Since Yorkshire hills are green,
Yet not in all the nests I meet
　　Can nightingale be seen.

Gathered from any wanderings,
　　Gethsemane can tell
Through what transporting anguish
　　She reached the asphodel!‡

Soft falls the sounds of Eden
　　Upon her puzzled ear;
Oh, what an afternoon for heaven,
　　When Brontë entered there!

CXXXVII

A toad can die of light!
Death is the common right

---

*Pen name of the English novelist Charlotte Brontë (1816–1855).
†Town in Yorkshire, a county in northern England where Brontë spent most of her life.
‡Plant in the lily family; in Greek poetry and mythology, the flower of Hades and the dead.

Of toads and men, —
Of earl and midge*
The privilege.
  Why swagger then?
The gnat's supremacy
Is large as thine.

CXXXVIII

FAR from love the Heavenly Father
  Leads the chosen child;
Oftener through realm of briar
  Than the meadow mild,

Oftener by the claw of dragon
  Than the hand of friend,
Guides the little one predestined
  To the native land.

CXXXIX

A long, long sleep, a famous sleep
  That makes no show for dawn
By stretch of limb or stir of lid, —
  An independent one.

Was ever idleness like this?
  Within a hut of stone
To bask the centuries away
  Nor once look up for noon?

---

*Gnatlike fly.

CXL

'T was just this time last year I died.
    I know I heard the corn,
When I was carried by the farms,—
    It had the tassels on.

I thought how yellow it would look
    When Richard went to mill;
And then I wanted to get out,
    But something held my will.

I thought just how red apples wedged
    The stubble's joints between;
And carts went stooping round the fields
    To take the pumpkins in.

I wondered which would miss me least,
    And when Thanksgiving came,
If father 'd multiply the plates
    To make an even sum.

And if my stocking hung too high,
    Would it blur the Christmas glee,
That not a Santa Claus could reach
    The altitude of me?

But this sort grieved myself, and so
    I thought how it would be
When just this time, some perfect year,
    Themselves should come to me.

CXLI

On this wondrous sea,
    Sailing silently,
Knowest thou the shore
    Ho! pilot, ho!
Where no breakers roar,
    Where the storm is o'er?

In the silent west
Many sails at rest,
    Their anchors fast;
Thither I pilot thee, —
Land, ho! Eternity!
    Ashore at last!

PART FIVE

THE SINGLE HOUND

ONE sister have I in our house,
And one a hedge away,
There's only one recorded
But both belong to me.

One came the way that I came
And wore my past year's gown,
The other as a bird her nest,
Builded our hearts among.

She did not sing as we did,
It was a different tune,
Herself to her a music
As Bumble-bee of June.

To-day is far from childhood
But up and down the hills
I held her hand the tighter,
Which shortened all the miles.

And still her hum the years among
Deceives the Butterfly,
Still in her eye the Violets lie
Mouldered this many May.

I spilt the dew but took the morn,
I chose this single star
From out the wide night's numbers,
Sue* —forevermore!

EMILY

---

*Susan Dickinson, Emily's friend and the wife of her brother, Austin.

I

ADVENTURE most unto itself
The Soul condemned to be;
Attended by a Single Hound—
Its own Identity.

II

THE Soul that has a Guest,
Doth seldom go abroad,
Diviner Crowd at home
Obliterate the need,
And courtesy forbid
A Host's departure, when
Upon Himself be visiting
The Emperor of Men!

III

EXCEPT the smaller size, no Lives are round,
These hurry to a sphere, and show, and end.

The larger, slower grow, and later hang—
The Summers of Hesperides* are long.

IV

FAME is a fickle food
Upon a shifting plate,
Whose table once a Guest, but not
The second time, is set.
Whose crumbs the crows inspect,
And with ironic caw
Flap past it to the Farmer's corn;
Men eat of it and die.

V

THE right to perish might be thought
An undisputed right,
Attempt it, and the Universe upon the opposite
Will concentrate its officers—
You cannot even die,
But Nature and Mankind must pause
To pay you scrutiny.

VI

PERIL as a possession
'T is good to bear,

---

*In Greek mythology, the garden of the Hesperides contained the golden apples
given to Hera as a wedding gift.

Danger disintegrates satiety;
There's Basis there
Begets an awe,
That searches Human Nature's creases
As clean as Fire.

VII

WHEN Etna* basks and purrs,
Naples is more afraid
Than when she shows her Garnet Tooth;
Security is loud.

VIII

REVERSE cannot befall that fine Prosperity
Whose sources are interior.
As soon Adversity
A diamond overtake,
In far Bolivian ground;
Misfortune hath no implement
Could mar it, if it found.

IX

To be alive is power,
Existence in itself,

---

*Mount Etna, a volcano in Sicily.

Without a further function,
Omnipotence enough.

To be alive and Will—
'T is able as a God!
The Further of ourselves be what—
Such being Finitude?

X

WITCHCRAFT has not a pedigree,
'T is early as our breath,
And mourners meet it going out
The moment of our death.

XI

EXHILARATION is the Breeze
That lifts us from the ground,
And leaves us in another place
Whose statement is not found;
Returns us not, but after time
We soberly descend,
A little newer for the term
Upon enchanted ground.

XII

No romance sold unto,
Could so enthrall a man

As the perusal of
His individual one.
'T is fiction's, to dilute
To plausibility
Our novel, when 't is small enough
To credit, — 't isn't true!

XIII

IF what we could were what we would —
Criterion be small;
It is the Ultimate of talk
The impotence to tell.

XIV

PERCEPTION of an
Object costs
Precise the Object's loss.
Perception in itself a gain
Replying to its price;
The Object Absolute is nought,
Perception sets it fair,
And then upbraids a Perfectness
That situates so far.

XV

No other can reduce
Our mortal consequence,

Like the remembering it be nought
A period from hence.
But contemplation for
Cotemporaneous nought
Our single competition;
Jehovah's estimate.

XVI

THE blunder is to estimate, —
"Eternity is *Then*,"
We say, as of a station.
Meanwhile he is so near,
He joins me in my ramble,
Divides abode with me,
No friend have I that so persists
As this Eternity.

XVII

My Wheel is in the dark, —
I cannot see a spoke,
Yet know its dripping feet
Go round and round.

My foot is on the tide —
An unfrequented road,
Yet have all roads
A "clearing" at the end.

Some have resigned the Loom,
Some in the busy tomb

Find quaint employ,
Some with new, stately feet
Pass royal through the gate,
Flinging the problem back at you and I.

XVIII

THERE is another Loneliness
That many die without,
Not want or friend occasions it,
Or circumstances or lot.

But nature sometimes, sometimes thought,
And whoso it befall
Is richer than could be divulged
By mortal numeral.

XIX

So gay a flower bereaved the mind
As if it were a woe,
Is Beauty an affliction, then?
Tradition ought to know.

XX

GLORY is that bright tragic thing,
That for an instant
Means Dominion,

Warms some poor name
That never felt the sun,
Gently replacing
In oblivion.

XXI

THE missing All prevented me
From missing minor things.
If nothing larger than a World's
Departure from a hinge,
Or Sun's extinction be observed,
'T was not so large that I
Could lift my forehead from my work
For curiosity.

XXII

HIS mind, of man a secret makes,
I meet him with a start,
He carries a circumference
In which I have no part,
Or even if I deem I do —
He otherwise may know.
Impregnable to inquest,
However neighborly.

XXIII

THE suburbs of a secret
A strategist should keep,

Better than on a dream intrude
To scrutinize the sleep.

XXIV

THE difference between despair
And fear, is like the one
Between the instant of a wreck,
And when the wreck has been.

The mind is smooth, — no motion —
Contented as the eye
Upon the forehead of a Bust,
That knows it cannot see.

XXV

THERE is a solitude of space,
A solitude of sea,
A solitude of death, but these
Society shall be,
Compared with that profounder site,
That polar privacy,
A Soul admitted to Itself:
Finite Infinity.

XXVI

THE props assist the house
Until the house is built,

And then the props withdraw—
And adequate, erect,
The house supports itself;
Ceasing to recollect
The auger and the carpenter.
Just such a retrospect
Hath the perfected life,
A past of plank and nail,
And slowness,—then the scaffolds drop—
Affirming it a soul.

XXVII

THE gleam of an heroic act,
Such strange illumination—
The Possible's slow fuse is lit
By the Imagination!

XXVIII

OF Death the sharpest function,
That, just as we discern,
The Excellence defies us;
Securest gathered then
The fruit perverse to plucking,
But leaning to the sight
With the ecstatic limit
Of unobtained Delight.

XXIX

DOWN Time's quaint stream
Without an oar,
We are enforced to sail,
Our Port—a secret—
Our Perchance—a gale.
What Skipper would
Incur the risk,
What Buccaneer would ride,
Without a surety from the wind
Or schedule of the tide?

XXX

I bet with every Wind that blew, till Nature in
    chagrin
Employed a *Fact* to visit me and scuttle my
    Balloon!

XXXI

THE Future never spoke,
Nor will he, like the Dumb,
Reveal by sign or syllable
Of his profound To-come.
But when the news be ripe,
Presents it in the Act—
Forestalling preparation
Escape or substitute.
Indifferent to him
The Dower as the Doom,

His office but to execute
Fate's Telegram to him.

XXXII

Two lengths has every day,
Its absolute extent —
And area superior
By hope or heaven lent.
Eternity will be
Velocity, or pause,
At fundamental signals
From fundamental laws.
To die, is not to go —
On doom's consummate chart
No territory new is staked,
Remain thou as thou art.

XXXIII

THE Soul's superior instants
Occur to Her alone,
When friend and earth's occasion
Have infinite withdrawn.

Or she, Herself, ascended
To too remote a height,
For lower recognition
Than Her Omnipotent.

This mortal abolition
Is seldom, but as fair

As Apparition—subject
To autocratic air.

Eternity's disclosure
To favorites, a few,
Of the Colossal substance
Of immortality.

XXXIV

NATURE is what we see,
The Hill, the Afternoon—
Squirrel, Eclipse, the Bumble-bee,
Nay—Nature is Heaven.

Nature is what we hear,
The Bobolink, the Sea—
Thunder, the Cricket—
Nay,—Nature is Harmony.

Nature is what we know
But have no art to say,
So impotent our wisdom is
To Her simplicity.

XXXV

AH, Teneriffe!*
            Retreating Mountain!
Purples of Ages pause for you,

---

*Tenerife (formerly Teneriffe) is the largest of the Canary Islands of Spain.

Sunset reviews her Sapphire Regiment,
Day drops you her red Adieu!

Still, clad in your mail of ices,
Thigh of granite and thew* of steel —
Heedless, alike, of pomp or parting,
Ah, Teneriffe!
          I'm kneeling still.

XXXVI

SHE died at play,
Gambolled away
Her lease of spotted hours,
Then sank as gaily as a Turk
Upon a couch of flowers.

Her ghost strolled softly o'er the hill
Yesterday and today,
Her vestments as the silver fleece,
Her countenance as spray.

XXXVII

"MORNING" means "Milking" to the Farmer
Dawn to the Apennines —
Dice to the Maid.
"Morning" means just Chance to the Lover —
Just Revelation to the Beloved.

---

*Muscle.

Epicures* date a breakfast by it!
Heroes a battle,
The Miller a flood,
Faint-going eyes their lapse
From sighing,
Faith, the Experiment of our Lord!

XXXVIII

A little madness in the Spring
Is wholesome even for the King,
But God be with the Clown,
Who ponders this tremendous scene—
This whole experiment of green,
As if it were his own!

XXXIX

I can't tell you, but you feel it—
Nor can you tell me,
Saints with vanished slate and pencil
Solve our April day.

Sweeter than a vanished Frolic
From a vanished Green!
Swifter than the hoofs of Horsemen
Round a ledge of Dream!

Modest, let us walk among it.
With our "faces veiled",

---

*People devoted to sensuous pleasure and luxurious living.

As they say polite Archangels
Do, in meeting God.*

Not for *me* to prate about it,
Not for *you* to say
To some fashionable Lady—
"Charming April Day!"

Rather Heaven's "Peter Parley",¹
By which, Children—slow—
To sublimer recitations
Are prepared to go!

XL

SOME Days retired from the rest
In soft distinction lie,
The Day that a companion came—
Or was obliged to die.

XLI

LIKE Men and Women shadows walk
Upon the hills today,
With here and there a mighty bow,
Or trailing courtesy
To Neighbors, doubtless, of their own;
Not quickened to perceive

---

*Throughout the Bible, beings confronting God do not look at him directly.
†*Peter Parley's Winter Evening Tales* (1829), by American writer Samuel Goodrich, was a popular book of didactic tales for children.

Minuter landscape, as Ourselves
And Boroughs where we live.

XLII

THE butterfly obtains
But little sympathy,
Though favorably mentioned
In Entomology.*
Because he travels freely
And wears a proper coat,
The circumspect are certain
That he is dissolute.
Had he the homely scutcheon† of modest Industry,
'T were fitter certifying for Immortality.

XLIII

BEAUTY crowds me till I die,
Beauty, mercy have on me!
But if I expire today,
  Let it be in sight of thee.

XLIV

WE spy the Forests and the Hills,
The tents to Nature's Show,

---

*Scientific study of insects.
†Escutcheon; a shield or shield-shaped emblem bearing a coat of arms.

Mistake the outside for the in
And mention what we saw.

Could Commentators on the sign
Of Nature's Caravan
Obtain "admission," as a child,
Some Wednesday afternoon?

XLV

I never told the buried gold
Upon the hill that lies,
I saw the sun, his plunder done,
Crouch low to guard his prize.

He stood as near, as stood you here,
A pace had been between—
Did but a snake bisect the brake,
My life had forfeit been.

That was a wondrous booty,
I hope 't was honest gained
Those were the finest ingots*
That ever kissed the spade.

Whether to keep the secret—
Whether to reveal—
Whether, while I ponder
Kidd† may sudden sail—

Could a Shrewd advise me
We might e'en divide—

---

*Blocks of metal, such as gold.
†William "Captain" Kidd (c.1645–1710), British sea captain and pirate.

Should a Shrewd betray me—
"Atropos"* decide!

XLVI

THE largest fire ever known
Occurs each afternoon,
Discovered is without surprise,
Proceeds without concern:
Consumes, and no report to men,
An Occidental town,
Rebuilt another morning
To be again burned down.

XLVII

BLOOM upon the Mountain, stated,
Blameless of a name.
Efflorescence of a Sunset—
Reproduced, the same.

Seed, had I, my purple sowing
Should endow the Day,
Not a tropic of the twilight
Show itself away.

Who for tilling, to the Mountain
Come, and disappear—

---

*In Greek mythology, three goddesses called the Fates controlled a person's life.
Clotho spun the thread of life; Lachesis measured its length; Atropos cut it.

Whose be Her renown, or fading,
Witness, is not here.

While I state—the solemn petals
Far as North and East,
Far as South and West expanding,
Culminate in rest.

And the Mountain to the Evening
Fit His countenance,
Indicating by no muscle
The Experience.

XLVIII

March is the month of expectation,
The things we do not know,
The Persons of prognostication
Are coming now.
We try to sham becoming firmness,
But pompous joy
Betrays us, as his first betrothal
Betrays a boy.

XLIX

The Duties of the Wind are few—
To cast the Ships at sea,
Establish March,
The Floods escort,
And usher Liberty.

L

THE Winds drew off
Like hungry dogs
Defeated of a bone.
Through fissures in
Volcanic cloud
The yellow lightning shown.
The trees held up
Their mangled limbs
Like animals in pain,
When Nature falls
Upon herself,
Beware an Austrian!

LI

I think that the root of the Wind is Water,
It would not sound so deep
Were it a firmamental product,
Airs no Oceans keep—
Mediterranean intonations,
To a Current's ear
There is a maritime conviction
In the atmosphere.

LII

So, from the mould,
Scarlet and gold

Many a Bulb will rise,
Hidden away cunningly
From sagacious eyes.
So, from cocoon
Many a Worm
Leap so Highland* gay,
Peasants like me—
Peasants like thee,
Gaze perplexedly.

LIII

THE long sigh of the Frog
Upon a Summer's day,
Enacts intoxication
Upon the revery.
But his receding swell
Substantiates a peace,
That makes the ear inordinate
For corporal release.

LIV

A cap of lead across the sky
Was tight and surly drawn,
We could not find the Mighty Face,
The figure was withdrawn.

---

*High or mountainous land, particularly the Highlands of central and northern Scotland.

A chill came up as from a shaft,
Our noon became a well,
A thunder storm combines the charms
Of Winter and of Hell.

LV

I send two Sunsets—
Day and I in competition ran,
I finished two, and several stars,
While He was making one.

His own is ampler—
But, as I was saying to a friend,
Mine is the more convenient
To carry in the hand.

(Sent with brilliant flowers.)

LVI

OF this is Day composed—
A morning and a noon,
A Revelry unspeakable
And then a gay Unknown;
Whose Pomps allure and spurn—
And dower and deprive,
And penury for glory
Remedilessly leave.

LVII

THE Hills erect their purple heads,
The Rivers lean to see —
Yet Man has not, of all the throng,
A curiosity.

LVIII

LIGHTLY stepped a yellow star
To its lofty place,
Loosed the Moon her silver hat
From her lustral* face.
All of evening softly lit
As an astral hall —
"Father," I observed to Heaven,
"You are punctual."

LIX

THE Moon upon her fluent route
Defiant of a road,
The stars Etruscan† argument,
Substantiate a God.
If Aims impel these Astral Ones,
The Ones allowed to know,
Know that which makes them as forgot
As Dawn forgets them now.

---

*Purifying.
†Relating to Etruria, an ancient country of west-central Italy.

LX

Like some old-fashioned miracle
When Summertime is done,
Seems Summer's recollection
And the affairs of June.

As infinite tradition
As Cinderella's bays,
Or little John* of Lincoln Green,
Or Bluebeard's† galleries.

Her Bees have a fictitious hum,
Her Blossoms, like a dream,
Elate—until we almost weep
So plausible they seem.

Her Memories like strains—review—
When Orchestra is dumb,
The Violin in baize‡ replaced
And Ear and Heaven numb.

LXI

Glowing is her Bonnet,
Glowing is her Cheek,
Glowing is her Kirtle,§
Yet she cannot speak!

---

*Companion of the legendary medieval hero Robin Hood.
†Character in a fairy tale by the French author Charles Perrault, who marries and then murders one wife after another.
‡Felt-like material, often bright green, used to cover gaming tables.
§Woman's long dress or skirt (archaic).

Better, as the Daisy
From the Summer hill,
Vanish unrecorded
Save by tearful Rill,*

Save by loving Sunrise
Looking for her face,
Save by feet unnumbered
Pausing at the place!

LXII

FOREVER cherished be the tree,
Whose apple Winter warm,
Enticed to breakfast from the sky
Two Gabriels yestermorn;
They registered in Nature's book
As Robin — Sire and Son,
But angels have that modest way
To screen them from renown.

LXIII

THE Ones that disappeared are back,
The Phoebe† and the Crow,
Precisely as in March is heard
The curtness of the Jay —
Be this an Autumn or a Spring?
My wisdom loses way,

*Small brook.
†North American bird.

One side of me the nuts are ripe—
The other side is May.

LXIV

THOSE final Creatures,—who they are—
That, faithful to the close,
Administer her ecstasy,
But just the Summer knows.

LXV

SUMMER begins to have the look,
Peruser* of enchanting Book
Reluctantly, but sure, perceives—
A gain upon the backward leaves.

Autumn begins to be inferred
By millinery of the cloud,
Or deeper color in the shawl
That wraps the everlasting hill.

The eye begins its avarice,
A meditation chastens speech,
Some Dyer of a distant tree
Resumes his gaudy industry.

Conclusion is the course of all,
Almost to be perennial,

---

*Examiner, reader.

And then elude stability
Recalls to immortality.

LXVI

A prompt, executive Bird is the Jay,
Bold as a Bailiff's hymn,
Brittle and brief in quality—
Warrant in every line;

Sitting a bough like a Brigadier,
Confident and straight,
Much is the mien
Of him in March
As a Magistrate.

LXVII

LIKE brooms of steel
The Snow and Wind
Had swept the Winter Street,
The House was hooked,
The Sun sent out
Faint Deputies of heat—
Where rode the Bird
The Silence tied
His ample, plodding Steed,
The Apple in the cellar snug
Was all the one that played.

LXVIII

THESE are the days that Reindeer love
And pranks the Northern star,
This is the Sun's objective
And Finland of the year.

LXIX

FOLLOW wise Orion
Till you lose your eye,
Dazzlingly decamping
He is just as high.

LXX

IN winter, in my room,
I came upon a worm,
Pink, lank, and warm.
But as he was a worm
And worms presume,
Not quite with him at home—
Secured him by a string
To something neighboring,
And went along.

A trifle afterward
A thing occurred,
I'd not believe it if I heard—
But state with creeping blood;

A snake, with mottles rare,
Surveyed my chamber floor,
In feature as the worm before,
But ringed with power.
The very string
With which I tied him, too,
When he was mean and new,
That string was there.

I shrank — "How fair you are!"
Propitiation's* claw —
"Afraid," he hissed,
"Of me?"
"No cordiality?"
He fathomed† me.
Then, to a rhythm slim
Secreted in his form,
As patterns swim,
Projected him.

That time I flew,
Both eyes his way,
Lest he pursue —
Nor ever ceased to run,
Till, in a distant town,
Towns on from mine —
I sat me down;
This was a dream.

LXXI

Not any sunny tone
From any fervent zone

---

*Propitiation is an act of appeasement or conciliation.
†Measured the depths of; understood.

Finds entrance there.
Better a grave of Balm
Toward human nature's home,
And Robins near,
Than a stupendous Tomb
Proclaiming to the gloom
How dead we are.

LXXII

FOR Death, — or rather
For the things 't will buy,
These put away
Life's opportunity.

The things that Death will buy
Are Room, — Escape
From Circumstances,
And a Name.

How gifts of Life
With Death's gifts will compare,
We know not —
For the rates stop Here.

LXXIII

DROPPED into the
Ether Acre!
Wearing the sod gown —
Bonnet of Everlasting laces —
Brooch frozen on!

Horses of blonde —
And coach of silver,
Baggage a strapped Pearl!
Journey of Down
And whip of Diamond —
Riding to meet the Earl!

LXXIV

THIS quiet Dust was Gentlemen and Ladies,
          And Lads and Girls;
Was laughter and ability and sighing,
          And frocks and curls.

This passive place a Summer's nimble mansion,
          Where Bloom and Bees
Fulfilled their Oriental Circuit,
          Then ceased like these.

LXXV

'T was comfort in her dying room
To hear the living clock,
A short relief to have the wind
Walk boldly up and knock,
Diversion from the dying theme
To hear the children play,
But wrong, the mere
That these could live, —
And This of ours must die!

LXXVI

Too cold is this
To warm with sun,
Too stiff to bended be,
To joint this agate* were a feat
Outstaring masonry.
How went the agile kernel out—
Contusion of the husk,
Nor rip, nor wrinkle indicate,—
But just an Asterisk.

LXXVII

I watched her face to see which way
She took the awful news,
Whether she died before she heard—
Or in protracted bruise
Remained a few short years with us,
Each heavier than the last—
A further afternoon to fail,
As Flower at fall of Frost.

LXXVIII

To-day or this noon
She dwelt so close,
I almost touched her;
Tonight she lies

---

*Fine-grained quartz with colored bands or clouding.

Past neighborhood—
And bough and steeple—
Now past surmise.

LXXIX

I see thee better in the dark,
I do not need a light.
The love of thee a prism be
Excelling violet.

I see thee better for the years
That hunch themselves between,
The miner's lamp sufficient be
To nullify the mine.

And in the grave I see thee best—
Its little panels be
A-glow, all ruddy with the light
I held so high for thee!

What need of day to those whose dark
Hath so surpassing sun,
It seem it be continually
At the meridian?*

LXXX

Low at my problem bending,
Another problem comes,

---

*Midday (archaic).

Larger than mine, serener,
Involving statelier sums;
I check my busy pencil,
My ciphers* slip away,
Wherefore, my baffled fingers,
Time Eternity?

LXXXI

IF pain for peace prepares,
Lo the "Augustan"† years
Our feet await!

If Springs from Winter rise,
Can the Anemone's
Be reckoned up?

If night stands first, then noon,
To gird us for the sun,
What gaze —

When, from a thousand skies,
On our developed eyes
Noons blaze!

LXXXII

I fit for them,
I seek the dark till I am thorough fit.

---

*Numbers; zeros.
†During the reign of the emperor Augustus (27 B.C.–A.D. 14), Rome enjoyed a flourishing of art and culture.

The labor is a solemn one,
With this sufficient sweet—
That abstinence as mine produce
A purer good for them,
If I succeed,—
If not, I had
The transport of the Aim.

LXXXIII

NOT one by Heaven defrauded stay,
Although He seem to steal,
He restitutes* in some sweet way.
Secreted in His will.

LXXXIV

THE feet of people walking home
In gayer sandals go,
The Crocus, till she rises,
The Vassal† of the Snow—
The lips at Hallelujah!
Long years of practice bore,
Till bye and bye these Bargemen
Walked singing on the shore.

Pearls are the Diver's farthings
Extorted from the Sea,

---

*Restores; reimburses.
†Subordinate or dependent.

Pinions* the Seraph's wagon,
Pedestrians once, as we—
Night is the morning's canvas,
Larceny, legacy,
Death but our rapt attention
To immortality.

My figures fail to tell me
How far the village lies,
Whose Peasants are the angels,
Whose Cantons† dot the skies,
My Classics veil their faces,
My Faith that dark adores,
Which from its solemn Abbeys
Such resurrection pours!

LXXXV

WE should not mind so small a flower,
Except it quiet bring
Our little garden that we lost
Back to the lawn again.
So spicy her Carnations red,
So drunken reel her Bees,
So silver steal a hundred Flutes
From out a hundred trees,
That whoso sees this little flower,
By faith may clear behold
The Bobolinks around the throne,
And Dandelions gold.

---

*Wings.
†Small territorial divisions of a country.

LXXXVI

To the staunch Dust we safe commit thee;
Tongue if it hath, inviolate to thee —
Silence denote and Sanctity enforce thee,
Passenger of Infinity!

LXXXVII

HER "Last Poems" —
Poets ended,
Silver perished with her tongue,
Not on record bubbled other
Flute, or Woman, so divine;
Not unto its Summer morning
Robin uttered half the tune —
Gushed too free for the adoring,
From the Anglo-Florentine.*
Late the praise —
'T is dull conferring
On a Head too high to crown,
Diadem or Ducal⁺ showing,
Be its Grave sufficient sign.
Yet if we, no Poet's kinsman,
Suffocate with easy woe,
What and if ourself a Bridegroom,
Put Her down, in Italy?

(Written after the death of Mrs. Browning in 1861.)

---

*The reference is to the English poet Elizabeth Barrett Browning (1806–1861),
who lived in Italy for many years.
†Relating to a duke or dukedom.

LXXXVIII

IMMURED* in Heaven! What a Cell!
Let every bondage be,
Thou Sweetest of the Universe,
Like that which ravished thee!

LXXXIX

I'M thinking of that other morn,
When Cerements† let go,
And Creatures clad in Victory
Go up in two by two!

XC

THE overtakelessness of those
Who have accomplished Death,
Majestic is to me beyond
The majesties of Earth.

The soul her "not at Home"
Inscribes upon the flesh,
And takes her fair aerial gait
Beyond the hope of touch.

---

*Enclosed, or imprisoned.
†Burial shrouds.

XCI

THE Look of Thee, what is it like?
Hast thou a hand or foot,
Or mansion of Identity,
And what is thy Pursuit?

Thy fellows, — are they Realms or Themes?
Hast thou Delight or Fear
Or Longing, — and is that for us
Or values more severe?

Let change transfuse all other traits,
Enact all other blame,
But deign this least certificate —
That thou shalt be the same.

XCII

THE Devil, had he fidelity,
Would be the finest friend —
Because he has ability,
But Devils cannot mend.
Perfidy is the virtue
That would he but resign, —
The Devil, so amended,
Were durably divine.

XCIII

PAPA above!
      Regard a Mouse

O'erpowered by the Cat;
Reserve within thy Kingdom
A "mansion" for the Rat!

Snug in seraphic cupboards
To nibble all the day,
While unsuspecting cycles
Wheel pompously away.

XCIV

NOT when we know
The Power accosts,
The garment of Surprise
Was all our timid Mother wore
At Home, in Paradise.

XCV

ELIJAH'S* wagon knew no thill,
Was innocent of wheel,
Elijah's horses as unique
As was his vehicle.
Elijah's journey to portray,
Expire with him the skill,
Who justified Elijah,
In feats inscrutable.

---

*Ninth-century B.C. Hebrew prophet who, according to the Bible, was carried skyward in a chariot of fire (see 2 Kings 2:11).

XCVI

"Remember me," implored the Thief—
Oh magnanimity!
"My Visitor in Paradise
I give thee Guaranty."

That courtesy will fair remain,
When the delight is dust,
With which we cite this mightiest case
Of compensated Trust.

Of All, we are allowed to hope,
But Affidavit stands
That this was due, where some, we fear,
Are unexpected friends.

XCVII

To this apartment deep
No ribaldry may creep;
Untroubled this abode
By any man but God.

XCVIII

"Sown in dishonor?"
Ah! Indeed!
May this dishonor be?
If I were half so fine myself,
I'd notice nobody!

"Sown in corruption?"
By no means!
Apostle is askew;
Corinthians 1:15, narrates
A circumstance or two!*

XCIX

THROUGH lane it lay, through bramble,
Through clearing and through wood,
Banditti† often passed us
Upon the lonely road.

The wolf came purring curious,
The owl looked puzzled down,
The serpent's satin figure
Glid stealthily along.

The tempest touched our garments,
The lightning's poignards‡ gleamed,
Fierce from the crag above us
The hungry vulture screamed.

The satyr's§ fingers beckoned,
The valley murmured "Come" —
These were the mates — and this the road
Those children fluttered home.

---

*1 Corinthians describes Christ's resurrection; the poem specifically refers to 1 Corinthians 15:42–43: "So also is the resurrection of the dead. It is sown in corruption; it is raised in corruption: it is sown in dishonour; it is raised in glory"(KJV).
†Bandits (Italian).
‡Daggers with slender blades.
§In Greek mythology, an immortal woodland goat-man given to unrestrained revelry.

C

Who is it seeks my pillow nights?
With plain inspecting face,
"Did you, or did you not?" to ask,
'T is Conscience, childhood's nurse.

With martial hand she strokes the hair
Upon my wincing head,
"All rogues shall have their part in" —
What —
        The Phosphorus* of God.

CI

His Cheek is his Biographer —
As long as he can blush,
Perdition is Opprobrium;
Past that, he sins in peace.
                        Thief

CII

"Heavenly Father," take to thee
The supreme iniquity,
Fashioned by thy candid hand
In a moment contraband.
Though to trust us seem to us

---

*Highly reactive nonmetallic element; a luminous substance.

More respectful—"we are dust."*
We apologize to Thee
For Thine own Duplicity.

CIII

THE sweets of Pillage can be known
To no one but the Thief,
Compassion for Integrity
Is his divinest Grief.

CIV

THE Bible is an antique volume
Written by faded men,
At the suggestion of Holy Spectres—†
Subjects—Bethlehem—
Eden—the ancient Homestead—
Satan—the Brigadier,
Judas—the great Defaulter,
David—the Troubadour.
Sin—a distinguished Precipice
Others must resist,
Boys that "believe"
Are very lonesome—
Other boys are "lost."
Had but the tale a warbling Teller
All the boys would come—

---

*Possibly an allusion to Old Testament passages: Job states that man's "foundation
is in the dust" (Job 4:19, KJV); Abraham claims that he is "but dust and ashes"
(Genesis 18:27, KJV).
†Ghostly apparitions; phantoms.

Orpheus'* sermon captivated,
It did not condemn.

CV

A little over Jordan,
As Genesis record,
An Angel and a Wrestler
Did wrestle long and hard.†

Till, morning touching mountain,
And Jacob waxing strong,
The Angel begged permission
To breakfast and return.

"Not so," quoth wily Jacob,
And girt his loins anew,
"Until thou bless me, stranger!"
The which acceded to:

Light swung the silver fleeces
Peniel‡ hills among,
And the astonished Wrestler
Found he had worsted God!

CVI

Dust is the only secret,
Death the only one

---

*In Greek mythology, a renowned poet and musician.
†In the Bible (Genesis 32:22–32), Jacob wrestles by the Jabbok River (a tributary of the Jordan) with an angel who turns out to be God.
‡Face of God.

You cannot find out all about
In his native town:
Nobody knew his father,
Never was a boy,
Hadn't any playmates
Or early history.

Industrious, laconic,
Punctual, sedate,
Bolder than a Brigand,*
Swifter than a Fleet,
Builds like a bird too,
Christ robs the next—
Robin after robin
Smuggled to rest!

CVII

AMBITION cannot find him,
Affection doesn't know
How many leagues of Nowhere
Lie between them now.
Yesterday undistinguished—
Eminent to-day,
For our mutual honor—
Immortality!

CVIII

EDEN is that old-fashioned House
We dwell in every day,

---

*Robber, or bandit.

Without suspecting our abode
Until we drive away.
How fair, on looking back, the Day
We sauntered from the door,
Unconscious our returning
Discover it no more.

CIX

CANDOR, my tepid Friend,
Come not to play with me!
The Myrrhs and Mochas* of the Mind
Are its Iniquity.

CX

SPEECH is a symptom of affection,
And Silence one,
The perfectest communication
Is heard of none —
Exists and its endorsement
Is had within —
Behold! said the Apostle,
Yet had not seen.

CXI

WHO were "the Father and the Son" —
We pondered when a child,

---

*Myrrhs are bitter resins used in perfume and incense; mochas are pungent Arabian coffees.

And what had they to do with us—
And when portentous told
With inference appalling,
By Childhood fortified,
We thought, "at least they are no worse
Than they have been described."

Who are "the Father and the Son"—
Did we demand today,
"The Father and the Son" himself
Would doubtless specify,
But had they the felicity
When we desired to know,
We better Friends had been, perhaps,
Than time ensue to be.

We start, to learn that we believe
But once, entirely—
Belief, it does not fit so well
When altered frequently.
We blush, that Heaven if we achieve,
Event ineffable—
We shall have shunned, until ashamed
To own the Miracle.

CXII

THAT Love is all there is,
Is all we know of Love;
It is enough, the freight should be
Proportioned to the groove.

CXIII

THE luxury to apprehend
The luxury 't would be
To look at thee a single time,
An Epicure of me,

In whatsoever Presence, makes,
Till, for a further food
I scarcely recollect to starve,
So first am I supplied.

The luxury to meditate
The luxury it was
To banquet on thy Countenance,
A sumptuousness bestows

On plainer days,
Whose table, far as
Certainty can see,
Is laden with a single crumb—
The consciousness of Thee.

CXIV

THE Sea said "Come" to the Brook,
The Brook said "Let me grow!"
The Sea said "Then you will be a Sea—
I want a brook, Come now!"

CXV

ALL I may, if small,
Do it not display

Larger for its Totalness?
'T is economy
To bestow a world
And withhold a star,
Utmost is munificence;
Less, though larger, Poor.

CXVI

Love reckons by itself alone,
"As large as I" relate the Sun
To one who never felt it blaze,
Itself is all the like it has.

CXVII

The inundation of the Spring
Submerges every soul,
It sweeps the tenement away
But leaves the water whole.
In which the Soul, at first alarmed,
Seeks furtive for its shore,
But acclimated, gropes no more
For that Peninsular.

CXVIII

No Autumn's intercepting chill
Appalls this Tropic Breast,

But African exuberance
And Asiatic Rest.

CXIX

VOLCANOES be in Sicily
And South America,
I judge from my geography.
Volcanoes nearer here,
A lava step, at any time,
Am I inclined to climb,
A crater I may contemplate,
Vesuvius* at home.

CXX

DISTANCE is not the realm of Fox,
Nor by relay† as Bird;
Abated, Distance is until
Thyself, Beloved!

CXXI

THE treason of an accent
Might vilify the Joy—

---

*Active volcano in southern Italy.
†Act of passing something along.

To breathe, — corrode the rapture
Of Sanctity to be.

CXXII

How destitute is he
Whose Gold is firm,
Who finds it every time,
The small stale sum —
When Love, with but a pence
Will so display,
As is a disrespect to India!*

CXXIII

CRISIS is sweet and, set of Heart
Upon the hither† side,
Has dowers of prospective
Surrendered by the Tried.
Inquire of the closing Rose
Which Rapture she preferred,
And she will tell you, sighing,
The transport of the Bud.

CXXIV

To tell the beauty would decrease,
To state the Spell demean,

---

*Perhaps an allusion to the opulence of Indian costumes.
†Near.

There is a syllableless sea
Of which it is the sign.

My will endeavours for its word
And fails, but entertains
A rapture as of legacies—
Of introspective mines.

CXXV

To love thee, year by year,
May less appear
Than sacrifice and cease.
However, Dear,
Forever might be short
I thought, to show,
And so I pieced it with a flower now.

CXXVI

I showed her heights she never saw—
"Wouldst climb?" I said,
She said "Not so"—
"With me?" I said, "With me?"
I showed her secrets
Morning's nest,
The rope that Nights were put across—
And *now*, "Wouldst have me for a Guest?"
She could not find her yes—
And then, I brake my life, and Lo!
A light for her, did solemn glow,

The larger, as her face withdrew—
And could she, further, "No?"

CXXVII

On my volcano grows the grass,—
A meditative spot,
An area for a bird to choose
Would be the general thought.

How red the fire reeks below,
How insecure the sod—
Did I disclose, would populate
With awe my solitude.

CXXVIII

If I could tell how glad I was,
I should not be so glad,
But when I cannot make the Force
Nor mould it into word,
I know it is a sign
That new Dilemma be
From mathematics further off,
Than from Eternity.

CXXIX

Her Grace is all she has,
And that, so vast displays,

One Art, to recognize, must be,
Another Art to praise.

CXXX

No matter where the Saints abide,
They make their circuit fair;
Behold how great a Firmament
Accompanies a star!

CXXXI

To see her is a picture,
To hear her is a tune,
To know her an intemperance
As innocent as June;
By which to be undone
Is dearer than Redemption —
Which never to receive,
Makes mockery of melody
It might have been to live.

CXXXII

So set its sun in thee,
What day is dark to me —
What distance far,
So I the ships may see

That touch how seldomly
Thy shore?

CXXXIII

HAD this one day not been,
Or could it cease to be—
How smitten, how superfluous
Were every other day!

Lest Love should value less
What Loss would value more,
Had it the stricken privilege—
It cherishes before.

CXXXIV

THAT she forgot me was the least,
I felt it second pain,
That I was worthy to forget
What most I thought upon.

Faithful, was all that I could boast,
But Constancy became,
To her, by her innominate,*
A something like a shame.

CXXXV

THE incidents of Love
Are more than its Events,

---

*Anonymous.

Investments best expositor
Is the minute per cents.

CXXXVI

A little overflowing word
That any hearing had inferred
For ardor or for tears,
Though generations pass away,
Traditions ripen and decay,
As eloquent appears

CXXXVII

JUST so, Jesus raps—He does not weary—
Last at the knocker and first at the bell,
Then on divinest tiptoe standing
Might He out-spy the lady's soul,
When He retires, chilled and weary—
It will be ample time for me;
Patient, upon the steps, until then—
Heart, I am knocking low at Thee!

CXXXVIII

SAFE Despair it is that raves,
Agony is frugal,
Puts itself severe away
For its own perusal.

Garrisoned no Soul can be
In the front of Trouble,
Love is one, not aggregate,
Nor is Dying double.

CXXXIX

THE Face we choose to miss,
Be it but for a day—
As absent as a hundred years
When it has rode away.

CXL

OF so divine a loss
We enter but the gain,
Indemnity for loneliness
That such a bliss has been.

CXLI

THE healed Heart shows its shallow scar
With confidential moan,
Not mended by Mortality
Are fabrics truly torn.
To go its convalescent way
So shameless is to see,
More genuine were Perfidy
Than such Fidelity.

CXLII

Give little anguish
Lives will fret.
Give avalanches —
And they'll slant,
Straighten, look cautious for their breath,
But make no syllable —
Like Death,
    Who only shows his
      Marble disc —
Sublimer sort than speech.

CXLIII

To pile like Thunder to its close,
Then crumble grand away,
While everything created hid —
This would be Poetry:
Or Love, — the two coeval came —
We both and neither prove,
Experience either, and consume —
For none see God and live.

CXLIV

The Stars are old, that stood for me —
The West a little worn,
Yet newer glows the only Gold
I ever cared to earn —
Presuming on that lone result

Her infinite disdain,
But vanquished her with my defeat,
'T was Victory was slain.

CXLV

ALL circumstances are the frame
In which His Face is set,
All Latitudes exist for His
Sufficient continent.

The light His Action and the dark
The Leisure of His Will,
In Him Existence serve, or set
A force illegible.

CXLVI

I did not reach thee,
But my feet slip nearer every day;
Three Rivers and a Hill to cross,
One Desert and a Sea—
I shall not count the journey one
When I am telling thee.

Two deserts—but the year is cold
So that will help the sand—
One desert crossed, the second one
Will feel as cool as land.
Sahara is too little price
To pay for thy Right hand!

The sea comes last. Step merry, feet!
So short have we to go
To play together we are prone,
But we must labor now,
The last shall be the lightest load
That we have had to draw.

The Sun goes crooked—that is night—
Before he makes the bend
We must have passed the middle sea,
Almost we wish the end
Were further off—too great it seems
So near the Whole to stand.

We step like plush, we stand like snow—
The waters murmur now,
Three rivers and the hill are passed,
'Two deserts and the sea!
Now Death usurps my premium*
And gets the look at Thee.

---

*Prize or reward.

INSPIRED BY EMILY DICKINSON'S POETRY

Dickinson is *the* American poet whose work consisted in exploring states of psychic extremity.

—Adrienne Rich

Poetry

"You who desired so much," begins Hart Crane's 1927 poem "To Emily Dickinson." He goes on to write: "Truly no flower yet withers in your hand." Emily Dickinson has kindled poetic fervor in writers for much of the twentieth century. Examples abound of poets who invite Dickinson into their poems and who, like Crane, personally address her. Adrienne Rich invokes Dickinson in her 1964 poem "I Am in Danger—Sir—," whose title comes from a letter Dickinson wrote to *Atlantic Monthly* editor Thomas Higginson. In another poem, "The Spirit of Place" (1981), Rich speaks of Dickinson's Amherst house: "This place is large enough for both of us / the river-fog will do for privacy / this is my third and last address to you." In "The Uses of Emily" (1986), the poet Maxine Kumin disparages "masculine critics" who give little heed to the women poets of their day, instead electing Dickinson as the safe choice, the "one woman worth mention." She goes on to note that Thomas Higginson was disdainful of Dickinson's poetry in the years just following her death.

Dickinson has served as an inspiration for countless poems, notably John Berryman's "Your Birthday in Wisconsin You are 140," Robert Bly's "Visiting Emily Dickinson's Grave with Robert Francis," Amy Clampitt's "Amherst," Archibald MacLeish's "In and Come In," Carl Sandburg's "Public Letter to Emily Dickinson," and William Stafford's "Emily." *Visiting Emily: Poems In-*

spired by the Life and Work of Emily Dickinson (Sheila Coghill and Thom Tammaro, eds., Iowa City: University of Iowa Press, 2000), an anthology of poems by more than eighty poets, celebrates the mystifying poet of Amherst and confirms her extraordinary influence on modern poetry.

Theater

Susan Glaspell's 1930 play *Alison's House* explores the lingering influence of a great poet, modeled after Emily Dickinson, on her family eighteen years after her death. As in much of her work, Glaspell focuses on the past as a source of strength and insight. In 1931 Glaspell received a Pulitzer Prize for *Alison's House*; she was the second woman ever to receive the Pulitzer. Throughout her career, Glaspell wrote thirteen plays, fourteen novels, and more than fifty short stories, articles, and essays.

Playwright William Luce delves into Dickinson's private life and thoughts in his one-woman play *The Belle of Amherst* (1976). The play focuses on the poet's passionate relationships with her childhood friends and her father, and Luce interweaves her poetry and epigrams into the script. *The Belle of Amherst* offers a unique glimpse into the mythologized psychology of Dickinson, particularly in regard to her strong motivation to write. The actress Julie Harris portrayed Dickinson in a 1976 Broadway performance of *The Belle of Amherst*. The show was filmed and aired on television, and Harris received her fifth Best Actress Tony Award for the role.

Dance

Can the life and poetry of Emily Dickinson be danced? For Martha Graham, the answer was an obvious yes. The acclaimed dancer and choreographer Martha Graham is remembered for her many innovations in modern dance; indeed, her name has become synonymous with the form. Her work *Letter to the World*, which premiered in 1940, takes its title from Dickinson's lines "This is my letter to the world, / That never wrote to me" (p. 5). Clad in a full, white gown reminiscent of the clothes Dickinson wore from her twenties on, Graham portrays the inner life of the poet — her torment, loss, and struggle to be happy. Barbara Morgan's well-known photograph of the performance captures Graham kicking her leg over her back, with her white dress swept up about her. Andy Warhol created a silkscreen print of the image entitled "Letter to the World (The Kick)." In her poem "Martha Graham in 'Letter to the World'" (2001), Lyn Lifshin writes, "Her words, a swirl of / her body."

Music

The passion and eccentricity of Dickinson's poetry translate well into music. Composers as diverse as Jan Meyerowitz, Vincent Persichetti, and Rudolf Escher have adapted Dickinson into their own symphonic poems. A work by Samuel Barber for a cappella chorus, "Let Down the Bars, O Death" (1936), is based on one of Dickinson's poems (p. 208). In 1950 Aaron Copland finished his work for voice and piano titled *Twelve Poems of Emily Dickinson*; his idiosyncratic approaches to each poem often mirror Dickinson's own erratic use of punctuation and language.

In 2001 Simon Holt composed *A Ribbon of Time*, a cycle of five pieces based on Dickinson's "I heard a fly buzz when I died" (p. 252). The second piece in the cycle, "Two movements for string quartet," won the 2002 Royal Philharmonic Society Music Award for Chamber-scale Composition; in the piece, the arrangements for the strings are spare and precise, creating a space for the buzzing fly, which is represented by a viola.

Visual Art

The power and simplicity of Dickinson's poems make her writing ideal raw material for visual artists. Her poetry has been incorporated into the works of such artists as Barbara Penn, Elaine Reichek, and Liz Rideal. In her paper sculptures, New York-based artist Lesley Dill uses a blend of exotic papers, including rice and metallic papers, to fashion dresses and necklaces reminiscent of Dickinson's customary attire; she then lithographs Dickinson's text onto the sculptures.

COMMENTS & QUESTIONS

In this section, we aim to provide the reader with an array of perspectives on the text, as well as questions that challenge those perspectives. The commentary has been culled from sources as diverse as reviews contemporaneous with the work, letters written by the author, literary criticism of later generations, and appreciations written throughout history. Following the commentary, a series of questions seeks to filter Emily Dickinson's Collected Poems *through a variety of points of view and bring about a richer understanding of these enduring works.*

Comments

SATURDAY REVIEW

The poems of Miss Emily Dickinson (who has hitherto been known to Englishmen chiefly if not only by some very injudicious praise of the kind usual with Mr. Howells) are posthumously published, and from the short preface written by her sympathetic and friendly editor we learn some interesting facts of her life. She appears never to have travelled, or, indeed, left the house of her father in Amherst, Mass., where she led the life of an absolute recluse, and only appeared in society at a yearly reception given by her father to his friends. We are told that she wrote verses abundantly, but "absolutely without the thought of publication, and solely by way of expression of the writer's own mind." The editor prepares us for the want of form and polish in her poems, but expects us to regard them as "poetry torn up from the roots, with rain and dew and earth still clinging to them, giving a freshness and a fragrance not otherwise to be conveyed." A merit is here implied in their very imperfections as producing the effect of poetry drawn from an absolutely natural unconventional source. We very much doubt, however, whether this conclusion may be fairly adduced from the uneducated and illiterate character of some of these verses, although we fully recognize in them the unmistakable touch of a true poet. In these days considerable mastery over form in poetry is not uncommon, but in our minor poets it is rare indeed to find much original thought, or a strongly marked individuality. For this reason it is, perhaps, difficult not to overvalue these qualities, when we find them, as in Miss Dickinson, separated from any merits of form. We continually see the thoughts of prose put into verse, but, while some of the poems in the present volume can scarcely be described as in verse at all, they almost all contain a genuinely poetical thought, or image, or feeling. Miss Dickinson's chief characteristics are, first, a faculty for seizing the impression or feelings of the moment, and fixing them with rare force and accuracy; secondly, a vividness of imagery, which impresses the reader as thoroughly unconventional, and shows considerable imaginative power. . . .

The editor suggests a comparison between the poems of this writer and those of William Blake; but, beyond the fact that they are both quite indifferent to the technical rules of art, the comparison is not very far-reaching. Miss Dickinson possesses little of that lyrical faculty to which Blake owes his reputation; but, on the other hand, she is gifted with a far saner mind. Her poems, however, may be said to be distinctively American in their peculiarities, and occasionally call to mind the verses of Emerson. The editor with his unfailing sympathy tells us that, "though curiously indifferent to all conventional rules," she yet had "a vigorous literary standard of her own, and often altered a word many times to suit an ear which had its own tenacious fastidiousness." Some of the poems, however, seem destitute of any metre whatever, the lines do not scan, the rhymes are arbitrarily thrown in or left out, in accordance with no fixed system, and grammar, and even good taste are only conspicuous by their absence. But in some of her roughest poems there is still an idea which forces the reader to attend to its meaning, and impresses him, in spite of the irritation he may feel at the form.

—September 5, 1891

THE NATION

The curious fame of [Emily Dickinson] is something unique in literature, being wholly posthumous and achieved without puffing or special effort, and, indeed, quite contrary to the expectation of both editors and publishers. No volumes of American poetry, not even the most popular of Longfellow's, have had so wide or so steady a sale. On the other hand, the books met with nothing but vehement hostility and derision on the part of leading English critics, and the sale of the first volume, when reprinted there, did not justify the issue of a second. The sole expressed objection to them, in the English mind, lay in their defects or irregularities of manner; and yet these were not nearly so defiant as those exhibited by Whitman, who has always been more unequivocally accepted in England than at home. There is, however, ample evidence that to a minority, at least, of English readers, Emily Dickinson is very dear. Some consideration is also due to the peculiarly American quality of the landscape, the birds, the flowers, she delineates. What does an Englishman know of the bobolink, the whippoor-will, the Baltimore oriole, even of the American robin or blue-jay? These have hardly been recognized as legitimate stock properties in poetry, either on the part of the London press or of that portion of the American which calls itself "cosmopolitan." To use them is still regarded, as when Emerson and Lowell were censured for their use, "a foolish affectation of the familiar." Why not stick to the conventional skylark and nightingale? Yet, as a matter of fact, if we may again draw upon Don Quixote's discourse to the poet, it is better that a Spaniard should write as a Spaniard and a Dutch-man as a Dutchman. If Emily Dickinson wishes to say, in her description of a spirit, " 'Tis whiter than an Indian pipe," let her say it.

—October 8, 1896

MARTHA HALE SHACKFORD

The secret of Emily Dickinson's wayward power seems to lie in three special characteristics, the first of which is her intensity of spiritual experience. Hers is the record of a soul endowed with unceasing activity in a world not material, but one where concrete facts are the cherished revelation of divine significances. Inquisitive always, alert to the inner truths of life, impatient of the brief destinies of convention, she isolated herself from the petty demands of social amenity. A sort of tireless, probing energy of mental action absorbed her, yet there is little speculation of a purely philosophical sort in her poetry. Her stubborn beliefs, learned in childhood, persisted to the end, — her conviction that life is beauty, that love explains grief, and that immortality endures. The quality of her writing is profoundly stirring, because it betrays, not the intellectual pioneer, but the acutely observant woman, whose capacity for feeling was profound. . . .

It is essentially in the world of spiritual forces that her depth of poetic originality is shown. Others may describe nature, but few can describe life as she does. Human nature, the experiences of the world of souls, was her special study, to which she brought, in addition to that quality of intensity, second characteristic, — keen sensitiveness to irony and paradox. Nearly all her perceptions are tinged with penetrating sense of the contrasts in human vicissitude. Controlled, alert, expectant, aware of the perpetual compromise between clay and spirit, she accepted the inscrutable truths of life in a fashion which reveals how humor and pathos contend in her. It is this which gives her style those sudden turns and that startling imagery. Humor is not, perhaps, a characteristic associated with pure lyric poetry, and yet Emily Dickinson's transcendental humor is one of the deep sources of her supremacy. Both in thought and in expression she gains her piercing quality, her undeniable spiritual thrust, by this gift, stimulating, mystifying, but forever inspiring her readers to a profound conception of high destinies.

The most apparent instances of this keen, shrewd delight in challenging convention, in the effort to establish, through contrast, reconcilement of the earthly and the eternal, are to be found in her imagery. Although her similes and metaphors may be devoid of languid aesthetic elegance, they are quivering to express living ideas, and so they come surprisingly close to what we are fond of calling the commonplace. She reverses the usual, she hitches her star to a wagon, transfixing homely daily phrases for poetic purposes. Such an audacity has seldom invaded poetry with a desire to tell immortal truths through the medium of a deep sentiment for old habitual things. It is true that we permit this liberty to the greatest poets, Shakespeare, Keats, Wordsworth, and some others; but in America our poets have been sharply charged not to offend in this respect. Here tradition still animates many critics in the belief that real poetry must have exalted phraseology. . . .

The expectation of finding in her work some quick, perverse, illuminating comment upon eternal truths certainly keeps a reader's interest from flagging, but passionate intensity and fine irony do not fully explain Emily Dickinson's significance. There is a third characteristic trait, a dauntless courage in accepting life. Existence, to her, was a momentous experience, and she let no promises of a future life deter her from feeling the throbs of this one. No false comfort released her from dismay at present anguish. An energy of pain and joy swept her soul, but did not leave any residue of bitterness or of sharp innuendo against the ways of the Almighty. Grief was a faith, not a disaster. She made no effort to smother the recollections of old companionship by that species of spiritual death to which so many people consent. . . . The willingness to look with clear directness at the spectacle of life is observable everywhere in her work. Passionate fortitude was hers, and this is the greatest contribution her poetry makes to the reading world. It is not expressed precisely in single poems, but rather is present in all, as key and interpretation of her meditative scrutiny. Without elaborate philosophy, yet with irresistible ways of expression, Emily Dickinson's poems have true lyric appeal, because they make abstractions such as love, hope, loneliness, death, and immortality, seem near and intimate and faithful.

—from *Atlantic Monthly* (January 1913)

Questions

1. Is it possible to abstract a consistent philosophy or religion or morality from Emily Dickinson's poetry?

2. What are the attributes of Emily Dickinson's God?

3.   That Love is all there is,
                           Is all we know of Love.

So wrote Dickinson in *The Single Hound* (page 312). Given all
that we know of her life, what do you think she meant by the word
"Love?" A relation to God? Charity and understanding for fellow
humans, or a sense of togetherness with them? Sex?

4. Take a poem by Dickinson that moves you. Scan it and the
prevailing meter is almost sure to be iambic (an unstressed syllable
followed by a stressed syllable). See whether the irregularities are
significant. In general, do you feel that there is a convergence of
form and content in her poems? After all, she has many subjects
but writes mostly within one form.

FOR FURTHER READING

Works by Dickinson

Letters. 3 vols. Edited by Thomas H. Johnson and Theodora Ward. Cambridge, MA: Harvard University Press, 1958. Based on the three-volume edition is the one-volume *Selected Letters,* edited by Thomas H. Johnson; Cambridge, MA: Harvard University Press, 1971. The 1971 edition is the source for most of the quotations in the Introduction to this edition. Dickinson's letters are an indispensable supplement to the poems.

The Manuscript Books of Emily Dickinson: A Facsimile Edition. Edited by R. W. Franklin. Cambridge, MA: Harvard University Press, 1981. Allows readers to see Dickinson's poems, and her frequent use of variant words, in her own hand.

The Master Letters of Emily Dickinson. Edited by R. W. Franklin. Amherst: University of Massachusetts Press, 1998.

The Poems of Emily Dickinson. 3 vols. Edited by Thomas H. Johnson. Cambridge, MA: Harvard University Press, 1955. This edition, with the poems arranged chronologically and the poet's idiosyncrasies intact, includes variant readings critically compared with all known manuscripts. A distillation of the three-volume edition is the one-volume *The Complete Poems of Emily Dickinson,* edited by Thomas H. Johnson (Boston: Little, Brown, 1976), which brings together the original texts of all 1,775 of Dickinson's poems. In the Introduction to this edition, quotations from poems not included in this edition are from the one-volume publication.

The Poems of Emily Dickinson. Edited by R. W. Franklin. Cambridge, MA: Harvard University Press, 1999. The most accurate version available today.

The University of Michigan Humanities Text Initiative, in its *American Verse Project*, contains poems from several editions of Dickinson's poems edited by Thomas Higginson and Mabel Loomis Todd (*Poems*, 1891, 1910, and 1914). (www.hti. umich.edu/index.html)

Biography

Farr, Judith. *The Passion of Emily Dickinson*. Cambridge, MA: Harvard University Press, 1992. Farr says that "although this book is not a biography, it attempts an inclusive vision of the poetry of Emily Dickinson, read in the context of her time, environment, and personal circumstances."

Habegger, Alfred. *My Wars Are Laid Away in Books: The Life of Emily Dickinson*. New York: Random House, 2001. Habegger writes that this book was written "with the feeling that it was time someone assess recent findings and claims relating to this poet."

Sewall, Richard B. *The Life of Emily Dickinson*. 1974. Cambridge, MA: Harvard University Press, 1994. Generally agreed to be the most thorough biography of the poet.

Wolff, Cynthia Griffin. *Emily Dickinson*. New York: Alfred A. Knopf, 1986. Particularly interesting for its psychoanalytic insights.

Context

Bennett, Fordyce R. *A Reference Guide to the Bible in Emily Dickinson's Poetry*. Lanham, MD: Scarecrow Press, 1997.

Capps, Jack L. *Emily Dickinson's Reading, 1836–1886*. Cambridge, MA: Harvard University Press, 1966.

Diehl, Joanne Feit. *Dickinson and the Romantic Imagination*. Princeton, NJ: Princeton University Press, 1981. Traces the influence of romantic poets on Dickinson's work.

Keller, Karl. *The Only Kangaroo Among the Beauty: Emily Dickinson and America*. Baltimore, MD: Johns Hopkins University

Press, 1979. Places Dickinson in the context of other American writers, from Anne Bradstreet to Robert Frost.

St. Armand, Barton Levi. *Emily Dickinson and Her Culture: The Soul's Society.* Cambridge and New York: Cambridge University Press, 1984. Solidly locates Dickinson in her time, exploring contemporary attitudes toward death, heaven, nature, etc.

Webster, Noah. *An American Dictionary of the English Language.* 1828. Reprint: New York: Johnson Reprint Corp., 1970.

Criticism

Bennett, Paula. *Emily Dickinson, Woman Poet.* Iowa City: University of Iowa Press, 1990.

Bogan, Louise, Archibald MacLeish, and Richard Wilbur. *Emily Dickinson: Three Views.* Amherst, MA: Amherst College Press, 1960. Three sensitive papers by poets, delivered at the Amherst Bicentennial in 1959.

Cameron, Sharon. *Choosing Not Choosing: Dickinson's Fascicles.* Chicago: University of Chicago Press, 1993. Cameron argues that Dickinson's manuscript variants should be treated as an essential part of the poems.

Farr, Judith, ed. *Emily Dickinson: A Collection of Critical Essays.* Upper Saddle River, NJ: Prentice Hall, 1996.

Fast, Robin Riley, and Christine Mack Gordon, eds. *Approaches to Teaching Dickinson's Poetry.* New York: Modern Language Association of America, 1989.

Ferlazzo, Paul J., ed. *Critical Essays on Emily Dickinson.* Boston: G. K. Hall, 1984.

Halio, Marcia Peoples, ed. *Emily Dickinson: A Collection of Poems.* Harcourt Brace Casebook Series in Literature. Fort Worth, TX: Harcourt College Publishers, 1998. This small book includes several of the best, most representative essays on Dickinson, as well as advice to students writing about her.

Howe, Susan. *My Emily Dickinson.* Berkeley, CA: North Atlantic Books, 1985. Perhaps the most personal book of criticism on Dickinson; Howe's exploration of Dickinson's variants and her lengthy interpretation of "My life had stood a loaded gun" (*The*

Complete Poems of Emily Dickinson, edited by Thomas H. Johnson, poem 754) are especially dazzling.

Kazin, Alfred. "Wrecked, Solitary, Here: Dickinson's Room of Her Own." In his *An American Procession*. New York: Alfred A. Knopf, 1984.

Martin, Wendy, ed. *The Cambridge Companion to Emily Dickinson*. Cambridge and New York: Cambridge University Press, 2002. Helpfully divided into sections biography and publication history, poetic strategies and themes, and cultural contexts.

Miller, Cristanne. *Emily Dickinson: A Poet's Grammar*. Cambridge, MA: Harvard University Press, 1987. Excellent.

Oberhaus, Dorothy Huff. *Emily Dickinson's Fascicles: Method and Meaning*. University Park: Pennsylvania State University Press, 1995.

Paglia, Camille. "Amherst's Madame de Sade: Emily Dickinson." In her *Sexual Personae: Art and Decadence from Nefertiti to Emily Dickinson*. New Haven: Yale University Press, 1990. Paglia asserts that "violence is her love song and lullaby."

Wolosky, Shira. *Emily Dickinson: A Voice of War*. New Haven: Yale University Press, 1984. Wolosky counters ahistorical readings of Dickinson by arguing that many of her poems are responses to the Civil War.

Modern Literature Inspired by Dickinson

Byatt, A. S. *Possession: A Romance*. New York: Random House, 1990.

Collins, Billy. *Picnic, Lightning*. Pittsburgh, PA: University of Pittsburgh Press, 1998.

Cope, Wendy. *Making Cocoa for Kingsley Amis*. London: Faber and Faber, 1986.

Crane, Hart. *The Poems of Hart Crane*. Edited by Marc Simon. New York: Liveright Publishing, 1986.

e. e. cummings. *e. e. cummings: Complete Poems 1904–1962*. Edited by George J. Firmage. New York: Liveright Publishing, 1994.

Farr, Judith. *I Never Came to You in White*. Boston: Houghton Mifflin, 1996.

Frost, Robert. *The Poetry of Robert Frost*. Edited by Edward Connery Lathem. New York: Holt, Rinehart and Winston, 1969.

Kalstone, David. *Becoming a Poet: Elizabeth Bishop with Marianne Moore and Robert Lowell*. New York: Farrar, Straus and Giroux, 1989. Contains remarks about Dickinson by Elizabeth Bishop.

Rich, Adrienne. *The Fact of a Doorframe: Selected Poems, 1950–2001*. New York: W. W. Norton, 2002.

Stevens, Wallace. *The Collected Poems*. New York: Vintage Books, 1982.

Williams, William Carlos. Interview in *Poets at Work: The Paris Review Interviews*, edited by George Plimpton. New York: Viking, 1989.

Other Dickinson Resources

Eberwein, Jane Donahue, ed. *An Emily Dickinson Encyclopedia*. Westport, CT: Greenwood Press, 1998. Contains entries on all aspects of Dickinson's life, culture, and work.

The Emily Dickinson International Society. The Society creates a forum for scholarship on Dickinson and her relation to the tradition of American poetry and women's literature. (www.cwru.edu/affil/edis/edisindex.html)

Grabher, Gudrun, Roland Hagenbüchle, and Cristanne Miller, eds. *The Emily Dickinson Handbook*. Amherst: University of Massachusetts Press, 1998. A source for quick reference containing basic and up-to-date information on the poet's life, her art, the manuscripts, and the current state of Dickinson scholarship.

INDEX OF FIRST LINES

Index of First Lines 345

B PAGE

Beauty crowds me till I die, ... 280
Because I could not stop for Death, ... 200
Before I got my eye put out, ... 39
Before the ice is in the pools, ... 251
Before you thought of spring, ... 84
Belshazzar had a letter,— 19
Bereaved of all, I went abroad, ... 244
Besides the Autumn poets sing, ... 111
Blazing in gold and quenching in purple, ... 107
Bless God, he went as soldiers, ... 240
Bloom upon the Mountain, stated, ... 282
Bring me the sunset in a cup, ... 105

C

Candor, my tepid Friend, ... 311
Come slowly, Eden! 163
Could I but ride indefinite, ... 142
Could mortal lip divine 56
Crisis is sweet and, set of Heart 316

D

Dare you see a soul at the white heat? 23
Dear March, come in! 135
Death is a dialogue between 202
Death is like the insect 237
Death sets a thing significant 214
Delayed till she had ceased to know, ... 187
Delight becomes pictorial 29
Departed to the judgment, ... 188
Did the harebell loose her girdle 169
Distance is not the realm of Fox, ... 315
Doubt me, my dim companion! 153
Down Time's quaint stream 274

I

PAGE

P

R   PAGE

S

Y
—